WAR READY

WAR READY

In My Father's Shadow

Mary Lou Darst

MARY LOU DARST

iUniverse

War Ready
In My Father's Shadow

iUniverse books may be ordered through booksellers or by contacting:

iUniverse
1663 Liberty Drive
Bloomington, IN 47403
www.iuniverse.com
1-800-Authors (1-800-288-4677)

ISBN: 978-1-4620-3154-2 (sc)
ISBN: 978-1-4620-3155-9 (hc)
ISBN: 978-1-4620-3156-6 (e)

Library of Congress Control Number: 2011909964

Print information available on the last page.

iUniverse rev. date: 12/01/2015

CONTENTS

I dedicate this book to American military families who have packed, pulled up stakes, said good-bye, moved, and started over again and again so that America could sleep peacefully at night.

With much love, I dedicate this book also to my brother Frank who followed me on this journey through life.

Thank you.

Acknowledgments

My thanks and deep gratitude to the following people, who were kind enough to read the manuscript in various stages and make suggestions and encouraging remarks. My wonderful editors—Mindy Reed, from Austin, Texas, and Nancy Hudson, from Missouri City, Texas—were invaluable, always available to answer questions, and razor-sharp in their assessments. Nancy also met with me and spent time talking about the book, which was very helpful. To the editors at iUniverse who saw the manuscript in ways that I never could, I am extremely grateful. To Peter Bowman, my partner, who so patiently encouraged me, listened to me, and without whose support I would never have written this book, I give my love and infinite thanks. I am especially indebted to my brother, Frank, who helped me write the Japan chapters by sharing stories and experiences I never knew. The book opened a door for conversations we'd never had before.

The technical support from Amy Baysinger, Laurie Lopez, and Jennifer Perez of Office Depot was above and beyond my expectations. The three girls made hundreds of manuscript copies for me to send to the reviewers. Amy was kind enough to complete the submission package while working long hours.

The following reviewers and readers offered invaluable observations, insights, encouragement, and comments. I am deeply indebted to Linda Gardner, Lex and Dana Ray, Inci Bowman, Beth Kingsley Hawkins, Cindy Wigg, Grace Martinez, Stephanie Visokay, and Terry Butterworth. I would also like to acknowledge my cousins Marcille Bruecher, Pat Bruecher, Jenn Hall, Sandra Sellers, Bertha Mary Stimac, Cathy Pearson—and her mother, Catharine Waldman, who was especially helpful—and my aunt, Jennie Lee Horton, who helped me early on with family history. The Book Club members Janice Hirsch, Ellen Lancaster, and Nancy Robinson were very helpful in their remarks. Each person's comments helped the book to grow and helped me to write better. The Galveston Writers, Nick Adams, Grace Clifford, Allen Griffen, Diana Dettling, and Debbie Stoutemire, were especially supportive and encouraging. Finally, Michelle Sierpina of Galveston, Texas, and the Osher Leisure Learning Institute (OLLI) at the University of Texas Medical Branch provided the groundwork for me to start writing. Michelle's generous support encouraged me to keep writing short stories. Alison Barker, the OLLI facilitator and my friend, listened to my short stories for four years, buffered sadness with comfort and love, and found positive things in every story. Special thanks go to Tom Bird of Sedona, Arizona, whose writing seminars allowed my inner child to feel safe, surface, and write.

In addition, my friend, Grace Martinez, sent the book as a gift to her friend, Jo Ann Clark, also a military dependent who attended Munich High School, but five years after I did. In turn, Jo Ann recommended the book to her friend, Dr. Karin Pohl, in Munich, Germany, who read it, and invited the author to Munich in October of 2012 to read from the book with the help of a translator for the **Americans in Munich Project**, which honors the contributions of Americans who lived in Munich between 1945 and 1992.

It is through the kindness of Karin Pohl that I have been able to reconnect after fifty-three years, with Helga and Gerhard, who with their parents, so generously opened their hearts to an American family in Munich from March 1957 to December 1959. How very fortunate I am!

Chronology

1943-45   My father was in England, Wales, and Scotland during WW II. After the war he was stationed in Coffeyville, Kansas, and later in Cheyenne, Wyoming, for two years before he was stationed in Fairbanks, Alaska.

1949-51   Fairbanks, Alaska

1950-52   Bellaire, Texas. My father was in Korea and then, later, Nara, Japan.

1952-54   Nara, Japan

1955-57   Lampasas, Texas

1957-59   Munich, Germany

1959   In December, we returned to the United States for the last time.

Introduction

I grew up as a military dependent, part of a family whose life was dictated by relocation orders from the US Army. As a result of our government's policy of policing the world after World War II, we traveled the globe, ready for change at a moment's notice, absorbing bits of new cultures wherever we lived. Transitioning to the past in order to document my early life was an emotional journey. I wept as I wrote about leaving my grandparents, aunts, uncles, and cousins. When I wrote about saying good-bye to people from other countries, whom I loved so much and who loved me equally, I wept again. But writing this book helped me grow as a person too. I looked back at the life of a child through the eyes of an adult. I gained a better understanding of my parents' reasoning for my brother and me. I saw their relationship from an adult's perspective, felt the fear they must have felt moving to Japan seven years after the war and then to Germany six years later. Writing about people like Mama-san, Hatsie, Mr. and Mrs. Kimoto, and Mr. and Mrs. Gruckenberg, whom I loved as much as I did my own grandparents, I realized that I saw the world through a different pair of eyes than my parents had.

Being a military dependent left me feeling that I do not belong in any one place. It was easy to make friends among military families because we all had so much in common—Americans away from home, displaced, but well traveled. There were wrenching, heartbreaking good-byes; fear of the unknown; fear that an American military uniform would provoke a negative response; and the simmering fear that we would not return to our families. But there were also joys: experiencing history firsthand as we did in Nara, living in an old Japanese house in downtown and having tea with Mama-san on Saturday mornings. Living in Munich, we traveled through Europe—taking in the Brussels World Fair; walking through the Coliseum in Rome, the streets of Pompeii, the Acropolis, and the streets of Tripoli, Libya; and shopping in the Grand Bazaar in Istanbul. There were new languages to learn, interactions with fascinating people, discoveries of similarities between our family and families in Asia and Europe. We also experienced the horrible realities of Hiroshima and Dachau. But despite all of these opportunities, coming home to our own family was the greatest joy.

It was not easy to live with my father, Carl Kennedy Hughes. He was away a lot, and by the time he came home, or we went to join him, we had all changed and were four strangers living under the same roof. He was always a soldier, a warrior, and he wanted us to be the same way. I never understood his rationale and have spent my life thinking about my father, wondering why he was the way he was and what made him that way. He was from Blytheville, Arkansas, and, to my knowledge, never traveled far from the area until he joined the Army Air Corps in 1940. While he was in England during the war, he was promoted from a sergeant to a second lieutenant and invited to join the Army Corps of Engineers. He was also "appointed a secret operations agent for the US government . . . concerning military sabotage, espionage . . . traitors, etc." (according to his WWII diary). My mother, Sara Catharine Emmott Hughes, was born in Houston, Texas. She also never traveled away from home until she married my father and military life took them both around the world.

My father did not see me until I was two years old. I was born in August 1943 in Houston while he was in a military camp on the East Coast preparing to go to war. In October 1943 he left Camp Kilmer, New Jersey, for the war in England. He did not return to Houston until November 1945.

Peeking through the shrubs in the back yard of my grandparents' house in Houston's West End, I saw my father for the first time. He got out of a shiny black car wearing a khaki uniform with short sleeves. When he came into the backyard, I asked who he was. He jerked around in surprise and looked at me for a long time before he replied, "My name is Carl Hughes." He stared at me a minute longer, then turned sharply, headed for the backdoor of the screened porch, and went inside. After a few minutes my grandmother came outside, smiling and happy. I asked her who that man was, and she said, "That man is your father!" At the time, I didn't know that I was supposed to have a father because my grandfather had filled that role. My father didn't stay at my grandparents' house very long, and when he left, my mother and I went with him. Two years later, my brother, Frank, was traveling with us.

Wherever we were, my father instilled in us that we were representing our country. Our behavior, including any verbal remarks we made, could easily be misinterpreted. We would not only embarrass our family and the United States military, but also give non-Americans the wrong impression of the United States, and although our behavior was exemplary at all times, I longed for his love.

I started writing this book for my grandsons, but when I revisited my childhood travels, I realized there may be some historical significance to the story. Here also was an opportunity to examine my past to learn what shaped me and how I became the person I am. I wanted to know more about my father, whom I never understood, and to explore our relationship. In doing so, I grew emotionally. The more I wrote, the more I began to realize that he was not only an engineer, but also a warrior who regarded everyone around him as a soldier. Was this a result of his WWII experience in England? No one can tell me now. Still, I am grateful for the travel experiences and the knowledge that the world does not begin and end at my front door.

1. Me at age two with my parents after my father returned from the war, in my grandparents' back yard
2. My parents in January 1943 in front of my aunt and uncle's house in Houston
3. My mother took me to visit my father's mother in Blytheville, Arkansas, while he was in England during the war. Here I am about 19 months.
4. Being held by my father after he returned from the war, in my grandparents' back yard
5. My dad working on a propeller in 1938

School Days
1948-49

1. Me with my great grandmother, Catharine Mary Elizabeth Taylor Emmott. She came from London in 1887. Taken while my father was in the war in London.
2. My father holding Frank with me in Alaska.
3. Frank and me in Alaska in front of our house in the winter snow.
4. My first grade picture.
5. My father with Frank and me in front of our house in the spring.

Alaska

After the war, my father was stationed in Coffeyville, Kansas, and then Cheyenne, Wyoming, where my brother, Frank, was born, and from there he was stationed in Fairbanks, Alaska, which was not yet part of the United States. We lived across from a forest so thick with trees, we couldn't see the interior even in the brightest sunshine, but we could hear wolves howling at night, which terrified this five-year-old. My mother often came into my bedroom and reassured me with lots of hugs that the wolves weren't going to come in and get us. Army housing—a three-bedroom duplex with hardwood floors, storm windows and doors, and a basement—was our home for eighteen months. The movers had already placed the army-issued furniture inside our new duplex; my father had seen to that before we arrived. But I missed my grandparents, aunts, uncles, and cousins more than anyone could possibly know.

No sooner had we settled in than I began to itch and couldn't stop scratching. Large red bumps appeared all over my body. Frank, eighteen months old, broke out with the same itchy red bumps. Several times a week, two nurses wearing dark blue capes, stiff white uniforms, and white caps with red crosses in the middle came to check on our progress. My mother applied calamine lotion to the itchy red bumps. Frank and I wore socks and mittens on our hands to keep from scratching. The chicken pox lasted about two weeks, but it took a little longer for all the scabs to dry up and fall off.

We had a number of unusual experiences while we lived in Alaska. One of the neighbors on the street behind us had a team of Huskies and a dog sled that he drove to the base every day. Sometimes the neighborhood children were treated to a dog-sled ride on Saturday afternoons. I was always afraid of the whip he used to move the dogs forward, although he never hit the dogs, only the snow-packed road. He talked to his dogs by yelling, "Mush! Mush!" Being the tallest, I stood at the back and held on to the sleigh while the other children sat in the front. Afterward, the dogs were friendly and enjoyed being petted. Their intense blue eyes and hairy tails attracted all the children.

One day my mother sent me on an errand across the street behind us. Remembering how friendly the dogs were when I was on the dogsled ride, I walked right up to the dogs so I could pet them—but they were eating. Before I knew it, those beautiful dogs turned on me—barking, growling, and jumping all over me. One of them bit me on the stomach. The owner's wife came out and calmed the dogs. Luckily, they all had current vaccinations. My mother applied iodine to the wound on my stomach, and it healed in time.

During the winter, it was dark most of the day and very cold. Icicles hung off the edge of the duplex, and we had to look carefully at the roof before entering and leaving the house. My father made deep tracks in the snow when he walked to the frozen dirt road behind our duplex for his early morning jeep ride to the base. When I was in the first grade, to reach the school-bus stop, I had to step carefully into each of his tracks to keep from getting stuck in the snow. In the afternoon when I came home from school, it was dark again, and I repeated the pattern. Snow stayed on the ground all winter, and one Saturday morning, my mother helped me put on my snowsuit and let me go out to play on the front sidewalk. The yard was covered in snow up to my shoulders. Although the sidewalk was fairly well cleared, it wasn't long before I fell off and got stuck.

"Mother, Mother! Come get me! I'm stuck! I can't move!" No response. I called again. "Mother, Mother!" No response. Thick white snow seemed to envelop me the way my grandparents used to hug me. Did my mother want me frozen like an icicle? Tears began to roll down my cheeks. My arms were stuck in the snow, and I couldn't wipe my face or my nose, which was running now. "Mother, Motherrr!" I started crying. She was inside with Frank. Did she not want me anymore? Is that why she let me come out and play in the snow, so I would get stuck and then freeze?" My grandmother wouldn't have let this happen. "Mother, Motherrr!" I cried louder, and I was getting colder.

She opened the door a little bit and stuck her head out. "What's the matter?" she asked.

"I'm stuck!" I cried. "I can't move! Come get me!"

"You don't look stuck," she responded.

"I'm stuck! I can't move! Come get me!" I shouted.

"All right," she said. "Just a minute, I have to put Frank in the playpen and put on my coat and boots. I need to get my mittens. Just a minute, I'll be right there. Don't cry, your tears might freeze on your face."

"Hurry up and come get me! I'm cold and I'm stuck!"

It seemed like forever before she opened the door again. Now she was bundled up from head to toe. From the sidewalk, she waded through the snow and pulled me out.

"How did you get so stuck?" she asked. "I told you just to play on the sidewalk."

"I don't know," I said tearfully. "I just kind of walked and fell and then I couldn't move."

We went inside, and she carefully wiped my nose and cheeks before removing my snowsuit and boots. Then she made some hot chocolate to warm me up. My grandmother would do that too, and I felt good again. I felt safe.

After my bath one night, my mother took me hurriedly into her bedroom to look out of the north window. She turned out the light and there I could see the magical movements of the aurora borealis. I was speechless. I pressed my face against the window to see every movement of this magic show, each color changing constantly.

"What is that?" I asked in astonishment.

"Those are the northern lights," my mother said.

I saw giant fingerlike forms made from millions of tiny colored lights woven together, creating a constant waving motion in front of a black velvet curtain.

"Can we see it every night?" I asked.

"No," my mother replied, "it doesn't appear all the time."

It was so beautiful and so unusual that I have never forgotten it.

On Thanksgiving Day, we dressed in our best clothes, and my father took us to a large hangar with tables and chairs set up inside. Thick white plates and military-issue silverware marked places on each long table. As we entered the hangar, familiar smells of Thanksgiving food greeted us. We sat at a table near the kitchen with some other people who only my father knew.

A woman wearing a fur coat spoke loudly, and everyone laughed, especially my father. She kept talking, and everyone kept laughing until my mother abruptly jumped up from the table with Frank in her arms and moved across the room to an empty table. My father took a drink of water and sent me to find out what was wrong with her.

My mother said she missed her parents and Grandmummy, her father's mother from England, as well as the holiday celebration she used to have with her family in Houston. She was especially sad during holidays. I wanted to see her happy and tried my best to make her laugh when she was sad. No one knew that I also missed being at home with our family. As I reported her response to my father, the lady with the loud voice stopped talking and everyone else stopped laughing. He sent me to tell my mother that he wanted her to come back to the table and be with him. In a few minutes my mother returned; although she ate in silence, her eyes never left my father's face. I commented that the mashed potatoes were really good, and everyone laughed. My father sent me to tell the sweaty, red-faced cooks about the potatoes. They were very pleased with my assessment of their cooking skills, and my father was very proud of me. As I recall, Frank and I were the only children present in the hangar for that Thanksgiving dinner.

I will never forget the Christmas we had in Alaska. When my mother came in to wake me up, it was still dark outside. I walked into the living room and couldn't believe my eyes. In a corner of the living room, there was a real Christmas tree covered with colored lights and beautiful ornaments. Underneath the tree were lots of packages wrapped in pretty paper with ribbons, and none of it had been there when I went to bed. My parents were very happy that morning, and Frank, who was two, was laughing at the things my mother gave to him. It was a wonderful morning. The surprise of finding a decorated Christmas tree with lots of presents underneath has stayed with me. I tried to recreate the same illusion for my own children every Christmas, but I'm afraid it was never quite like my memory of the holiday in Alaska.

Santa left me a set of *My Book House* books, which I still have. The twenty books are a collection of children's stories from around the world, including nursery rhymes and young-adult literature. I loved the illustrated stories with Victorian pictures. My mother used to read stories to me every night when we lived in Alaska. I loved the blue leather covers and the large Victorian picture on the front of each book, an illustration from one of the stories. As I grew up, I continued reading the stories that were age appropriate. I read to my children from the same books. My son especially enjoyed the stories from these books.

Behind our duplex there was a playground with a see-saw and a swing set for neighborhood children. Sometimes in the afternoon my mother gave me permission to go swing while she watched me from the kitchen window. Once as I stood pumping away, I could feel vibrations from the swing set through my shoes and my hands. A deafening tornado-like roar drowned out all other sounds. Suddenly, the earth began shaking violently; everything around me was shaking. I held on for dear life, not knowing that it was an earthquake. I was thrown up high out of the swing, over the top of the swing set, but I blacked out when I hit the ground. Later, I opened my eyes to find my mother leaning over me, screaming my name. My father stood on the concrete stoop at the back of the duplex and watched while keeping Frank inside.

Not long afterward, the tornado-like roar came again without warning while we were sitting at the dining room table. My mother's eyes grew large as she glanced quickly at my father. With a smile he simply said, "Just hold on to the table. There's nothing we can do about this because everything else is shaking too." The dishes vibrated in circles and the silverware vibrated up and down while the table was shaking, but nothing fell off. The house shook so violently, it felt like the duplex was moving off of its foundation. We held onto the table, but to our relief, the duplex did not move.

Periodically, my father invited some of the officers from the base to our house for dinner. They always wore their green army uniforms when they came. My mother put on a pretty dress and smiled a lot while she moved from the kitchen to the dining room. No one was aware that she had spent several days preparing for their visit. I entertained my brother for long periods of time so she could complete the preparations. My father was very proud of my mother and liked to show her off. My parents always entertained a lot, and were included in many military social events.

We did not have a car and there was no bus service, which made getting to the commissary to buy groceries difficult for my mother. In addition, she had an active two-year-old. My father brought groceries home in a covered three-quarter-ton army truck. Some of the men who worked for him unloaded the cardboard boxes, which were filled with groceries, including powdered milk, and stacked them on the kitchen floor. My mother was grateful for the groceries, but before she could begin to put anything away, she had to mop up the melted snow and muddy dirt that the men had tracked onto the kitchen floor.

Our luggage was stored in the basement with a wringer washing machine. I loved to go to the basement with my mother and watch the clothes come out of the wringer. Sometimes she even let me feed the clothes into it. Frank loved to run around in the basement and look for bits of dirt or insects. When the clothes had finished washing, my mother carried all the clothes upstairs to the backyard and hung them on the line, even when it was cold. In the dead of winter, she hung the clothes in the basement and in the kitchen to dry.

Sometimes my father took me to the barber shop to see the Eskimos who cut hair for the soldiers. Compared to my family, they were short and their skin was brownish-red. Their eyes were slanted with the epicanthic lid in contrast to our more rounded look. They were quiet and focused on cutting the hair of their customers.

He also took me to a hangar to see the enormous earth-moving machinery he used in Fairbanks. He hopped up on a yellow road grader, turned on the engine, and wanted me to come up and sit beside him. The noise from the engine was deafening. I stood in my Sunday dress—a wool coat with a white muff, patent-leather shoes, and lace socks—frozen to the ground. Finally, one of the soldiers standing nearby lifted me up into my father's arms. I sat close to his right leg until he turned the engine off and handed me down to the same soldier. He seemed very proud to have me sitting close to him. I felt very secure and much loved, although frightened by loud noises and vibrations of the huge machine.

Long summer days and the warm stream of Pacific water produced an abundance of fresh fruits and vegetables along the coast. During the summer, we took a drive to the coast to pick strawberries, my favorite fruit. It was a wonderful day. I ran up and down rows of small green plants, unsupervised in my bare feet, picking one strawberry to eat and one to put in my basket. My father said, "Mary Lou, put some strawberries in the basket."

During the middle of the summer, we had daylight for twenty-four hours. My mother put army blankets over our bedroom windows to create darkness, not only so we could sleep, but so my parents could sleep as well. Before she started using blankets to make our rooms dark, we played late at night and did not show any signs of being sleepy or tired.

Neighbors gathered behind the duplexes one afternoon, taking in the beauty of a natural wonder, a mother-of-pearl cloud, as it floated slowly across the sky. A pale pink cloud, with pastel colors of the rainbow along the edge, covered the entire sky. This phenomenon appeared about every forty years, according to my mother. Many of the women in the neighborhood were wearing shorts, and nearly everyone was taking pictures.

Nothing made my mother as sad as the news that Grandmummy had died. She'd lived behind my grandparents in Houston's West End. My mother cried all day, and I thought she would never stop. There was a huge mountain of clean laundry on the sofa. While she wept, she kept trying to fold all the clothes and kept asking me if I wanted to go home and live with my grandparents. I rode my tricycle around and around the sofa and said, "Yes," thinking that we could go home that minute, but we didn't. She didn't make much progress folding the clothes. Late in the afternoon she just gave up, put the wrinkled clothes back in the laundry basket, took her afternoon bath, and started our supper. Not long after this sad day, it was time to move again.

Frank and me in front of the Shirley Duke apartments in Alexandria, Virginia.
That is our black Dodge in the background. I was seven and Frank was three.

1. My mother had this picture taken of us to send to my father in Korea or Japan.
2. Frank, my mother, and me in front of my grandparents' house shortly after we arrived from Alexandria, Virginia.
3. Frank at Christmas with Mimi and Pepaw when my father was in Japan. My grandparents, Bertie and Edgar Emmott in their living room.

Alexandria, Virginia

In 1951, the Korean War was simmering. The thirty-eighth parallel became the dividing line between Chinese troops who occupied the north and American troops who occupied the south. Since my father was an army officer and an engineer, would this new conflict involve him too? We followed him around the world, but Frank and I were sheltered from knowledge of his assignments and the work he performed. We knew only of impending changes to our location. After living in Alaska, we headed back to Houston for a long visit with my grandparents. My father went to Fort Belvoir, Virginia, where he attended engineering school as part of his assignment. We joined him in Virginia when he found an apartment in Shirley Duke, a suburb of Alexandria.

We said good-bye to my mother's family in Houston and arrived in Virginia by train. My father hugged and kissed my mother warmly and marveled at my brother's growth. He hugged Frank and held him close to his chest telling my mother what a good job she had done with him. I waited anxiously and quietly for a hug and some word of praise as my father handed my brother back to my mother, but he only frowned at me and looked away while my mother looked at me and then at my father. I stood in front of him with a smile frozen on my face. I was wearing the new dress my mother had made, new patent-leather shoes, and white lace socks, hoping that he might notice me. I longed for him to embrace me. Instead, with his jaw set, a scowl formed on his face and he grabbed our large suitcase. "Let's get going," he said, and started moving toward the bus, all the while ignoring me. I was unbelievably hurt, and I couldn't understand why my father wasn't glad to see me. He hadn't lived with us for almost a year. I wondered what I had done.

The bus ride to our apartment was more difficult. I sat in front of my parents and Frank, because my father didn't want me to sit with him. I felt completely misplaced and wondered why I had to be on the bus with this man, my father. A single woman sat down beside me. When she smiled at me, I was so relieved that I began to talk to her, telling her all the things I had saved to tell my father. He was not pleased with this at all. He glared at me and, in a loud voice, told me to stop talking. Everyone around us turned and looked at him and at me. I couldn't believe that he had yelled at me. My grandfather never yelled at me; nobody ever yelled at me. I was hiding all the hurt I was feeling by talking, talking, talking. Then I felt a hard slap on my shoulder. When I looked back at him, his eyes were burning and his face was red. He was glaring harder at me, and his hand was poised to hit again. I turned away quickly and looked out of the window with watery eyes and a burning shoulder. Who was this man I called father? Why was I supposed to love him? Why did I have to live with him? Where was the man who wanted me to sit next to him on the large yellow road grader in Alaska? Why did he act this way toward me? What had I done? This was an indication of our developing relationship, but I'm still at a loss as to what triggered this change in my father. I have no clue why he did not want me around, why I created such a negative reaction in him. It was in Alexandria that he started calling me stupid. "How could anybody be that stupid!" he shouted when I didn't respond the way he thought I should. He would shake his head and laugh at my stupidity. I was so humiliated. I felt like such a failure. I didn't want anyone to know that my father called me stupid, that he thought of me as stupid. Thankfully, he only did this when we were at home.

I realize now that he was a warrior and a soldier before he was anything else, and he wanted his family to be that way too. He wanted us to be independent and to stand on our own two feet. His attitude toward me made life very difficult for my mother.

She was in a constant tug of war trying to be a good military wife and protecting me from my father's verbal attacks. As Frank grew older, she tried to protect both of us. Although she loved my father very much, she spent her life trying to shelter us from his harsh verbal remarks and his sometimes physical manner.

Our weekends in Alexandria were filled with sightseeing in the area, especially the cherry blossoms near the Jefferson Memorial in the spring, the Reflecting Pool, and the Lincoln Memorial in Washington, DC. Some weekends we drove to Union Station to watch the steam engines passing in and out of Alexandria. A number of times we drove to National Airport to watch planes take off and land. One of the most interesting places we visited was the C&O (Chesapeake and Ohio) canal. It had a series of locks and a wide brick road on each side, built for mules to pull boats loaded with goods.

Sometimes on a sunny weekend day my mother fried chicken and packed a picnic lunch. My father loved to be outside. He drove us out into the Virginia countryside until there were no signs of civilization. We rolled down the windows, listened to the birds, and looked for a clearing to spread our army blankets so we could get out and eat. We returned home a different way so the landscape was always changing for us. Those were happy times, but they were short-lived.

The public school in Shirley Duke was in a converted apartment building where I attended second grade on the second floor. I walked to and from school every day, and sometimes I walked home for lunch. My mother gave me a quarter every week to buy part of a US savings bond through the school. Our teacher played patriotic music while we pasted these stamps in a special book issued to each student. We also practiced sheltering ourselves from an atomic bomb attack. We crawled under our desks or along the wall, away from the windows, holding our heads down, placing one arm over the back of our necks. While I was at school, Frank played cowboys and Indians with neighborhood children in the back of the apartment building or dug in the sandbox there. My mother joined the few stay-at-home mothers who gathered on park benches and watched their children play.

After we had been in the apartment for a few months, my parents bought a small television set with rabbit ears on top. On Saturday nights we were allowed to stay up and watch Imogene Coca and Sid Caesar on *Your Show of Shows*, which kept us all laughing. During the day, my mother left our small radio on. "Beetle Bomb" was Frank's favorite song, and whenever he heard it, he stood by the radio and shook with laughter. I saw the televised hydrogen bomb test in the Nevada desert with my mother; the enormous mushroom cloud, the waves of energy that destroyed buildings built just for the test. She talked about how dangerous it was and how it could harm so many people. Neither of us realized at the time how significant these pictures would come to be in our future.

Persistent upper respiratory infections convinced my parents to have my tonsils removed while we lived in Alexandria. My mother was with me as I was prepared for surgery. She was invited to come into the operating room with me, wearing a nice dress, stockings, high-heeled shoes, and her good winter coat. The anesthesiologist showed me the black mask he was going to put over my face to make me go to sleep, but I was afraid. He put the mask up to his face and then to my mother's face. She encouraged me to take a deep breath when he covered my face with it. I did, and the ether put me to sleep immediately. After the tonsils were removed, I was free from colds and tonsillitis.

On Christmas morning Frank and I woke up to a decorated Christmas tree with presents underneath like we did in Alaska. Frank was delighted to have toys with wheels that moved easily. Santa brought me a Madame Alexander doll and a doll trunk filled with beautiful doll clothes. My father's handwriting was on the trunk tag: "To Mary Lou, From Santa." The doll clothes were rich with detail: lace, tiny buttons, pleats, and ribbons. When we moved they were packed away in storage with Franks' cars and trucks. The next time I saw them, I had a seven-year-old daughter and wanted her to enjoy them as I had. When I opened the doll trunk, my mother told me she had made the doll clothes. They were so beautiful, I couldn't believe it. My daughter was delighted with the unexpected gift. When we arrived at our home in Galveston, she opened the doll trunk and started dressing

Paddypaws, our cat, in the beautiful doll clothes my mother had made for my doll. Paddypaws was a gentle cat and didn't mind being dressed at all. In fact, the doll clothes were quite attractive on her. I still have the doll trunk, the doll, and all the clothes in my attic.

Whenever we moved, the army provided professional movers to pack all of our belongings, which were put into storage until our return to the States. The dolls spent most of my life and theirs in storage, as did Frank's toys. When we traveled, Frank and I always had coloring books, crayons, playing cards, and some books to read. We usually gave things such as clothes, shoes, and toys to the neighbors before my mother started packing. We watched with sadness and excitement when the movers came, removing our possessions packed in large wooden boxes, nailed shut, and stenciled with my father's name, rank, serial number, and a forwarding address. Feelings of anxiety and isolation began to build as the furniture was removed from our apartment, clothes were packed in the suitcases, and we were left with only the remnants of our former life. We would have some time with our grandparents in Houston, but then what lay ahead? Where would we live next? How long before we would have our things again? This pattern would be repeated again and again until my father retired from the service. When we were older, Frank and I each had one footlocker for packing our own personal possessions, but first we had to let go of a lot of things.

My father returned the apartment key to the manager, and we headed to Houston for a long stay with my grandparents—but first we stopped in Blytheville, Arkansas, to visit my father's mother and family. While there for only a long weekend, we went with my aunt and cousins to watch the "darkies" picking cotton. We stood near a large field of small plants covered in white that my mother explained were cotton plants. Standing at the end of each row of plants, Negro men placed a large burlap bag over one shoulder. The bags draped on the ground near the feet of each man. Only a few of the men wore shoes; the others were barefooted. I heard a gunshot, and the men jumped to the plants, their hands moving quickly, stripping the cotton from each plant, depositing it in their bag, and moving hurriedly to the next plant. They seemed to be doing a dance, bending over the plants, hands moving from the small plants to the large bags dragging in the dirt, and then back to the plants. Each dark body was in constant motion as the white cotton disappeared into the dirty burlap bags. As the men worked over each plant, small bits of cotton lay in the dirt around the plants and in the rows where they walked. They picked and moved so fast their hands blurred as I stood watching them. As the men worked halfway down the rows of plants, the burlap bags filled with cotton began to drag in the dirt, and the men strained to pull them forward. It was hot and humid outside. As the men moved closer to us, I could see perspiration pouring off of them, even though some wore a bandana around their head or neck. Some of the men wore large straw hats. Others wore suspenders to hold up their loose-fitting pants. I did not understand why the men were picking cotton this way, why they had to rush, or why they didn't stop to stand up or get a drink. My mother explained that it was a contest and the men were racing to see who could finish first. She said they would get water and rest when the contest was over.

We saw many of my father's cousins at a large dinner my grandmother prepared. This was the first time I could remember meeting so many of my father's relatives. Frank and I were well fed and well hugged by the time we were ready to leave.

My grandmother and my aunt, who lived next door, gave my parents pickled beets, fresh squash, and cucumbers from their garden, along with homemade jellies in mason jars. My mother was especially delighted with this gift. As we walked to the car and loaded our traveling books, fresh vegetables, and jellies, my father hugged his mother warmly. Grandma hugged my mother, Frank, and me and told each of us that she loved us. As we got in the car, she hugged my father again, holding him close to her ample body. In a moment, he turned away without saying anything, got in the car, put on his sunglasses, and started the engine. He turned the car around slowly and drove past my grandmother at a snail's pace without smiling or waving, just staring. We waved through the open windows as she waved back at us. My father lit a cigarette and took a long drag while we watched Grandma out of the back window, growing smaller and smaller as we drove away.

It took us two long days to reach Houston. Once again we were all well hugged and well fed at my grandparents' house by cousins, aunts, and uncles. We had been living with my grandparents in Houston for about a week when I woke up very early and saw the living room light on. It was still dark outside, and I dressed quickly, curious about what was happening in the house. I peeked in the living room and saw that all the lamps were on. My parents were standing by the front door. My mother was crying softly, and her face was red as if she had been crying for a while; she was staring at my father, her hands resting on his shoulders. My father, wearing his summer khakis, held her gently in his arms and stared at her as if they were the only ones in the house. He spoke to her softly, holding her with his hands on her waist. I had never seen my parents in this posture. Fascinated with the tenderness that passed between them, I stood in the doorway watching, wondering why my parents were standing in front of the door that way. I wanted to be part of the tenderness. Maybe my father could be gentle toward me too. I walked quietly into the living room and stood next to them with a big smile on my face, anxious for their approval. Now I understood. My father was leaving again. I didn't know where he was going, but I wanted to say good-bye to him. I wanted to experience a tender side of him. But when I said, "Bye, Daddy," they both jumped. "Mary Lou!" my father bellowed, and I jumped. My mother's eyes never left his face, but my grandmother appeared suddenly from the kitchen and said loudly, "Good-bye, Carl." He never took his eyes off my mother's face, as he quietly said, "Good-bye," opened the front door, and left. As the door closed I realized what a mistake I had made. Why didn't I just stand in the hallway and watch? Now it was too late to say, "I'm sorry," or ask my father why he was leaving again. Perhaps my mother wept for some time, but I stayed in the kitchen with my grandmother watching the sun come up until my mother came in, looking very sad and downcast.

*   *   *

"Frank, what's in the bottom drawer of Daddy's desk? I've emptied the top drawers, but now I need to put a load in the car. I'm getting hungry too. Why don't we go eat after you empty that last drawer?"

"Mary Lou. We will never get through with this if you need to go put something in the car every ten minutes. How can you still be hungry? You just had some donuts at ten o'clock. It's now eleven o'clock. We will be through cleaning out Daddy's things by the end of the day. We still have to go through his closet. Calm down."

"Okay. Be back in a few minutes."

When I returned, Frank had emptied the bottom drawers in our father's desk and his dresser. He placed everything on our parents' king-sized bed for easier viewing.

"Look at this," he said, seriously. "Look at this."

"Look at what? All those papers? What does that one say?" I asked.

"It says Daddy served honorably in Korea. Here are some medals to go with it." Stunned into silence, we sat staring at the certificate and the medals.

"Frank, I never knew he went to Korea. I thought he went to Japan, to Nara, where we lived for eighteen months."

"I never knew either, but remember, he was gone for over a year while we lived with Mimi and Pepaw." ("Mimi and Pepaw" meaning our grandparents.)

"Yes, I remember, but why didn't they tell us where he was going? What was he doing while he was there?"

"He was an engineer. That's all we know."

We sat on the bed and stared in silent disbelief at the evidence of his duty in Korea. Even after we had joined him in Nara, nothing had ever been mentioned about my father's assignment in Korea. After his death, Frank and I found his ribbons, medals, and certificates noting his assignment there. Was it a secret assignment? Neither of our parents ever spoke about it.

*   *   *

Because I was the oldest, I felt it was my place to look after my mother and my brother when my father was away, but at my grandparents' house, I could relax because we were living with her parents. Her brothers and sisters also lived in Bellaire, a suburb of Houston. There was always someone for her to talk to, and there were lots of cousins for Frank and me to play with.

In the spring of 1952, the polio epidemic in Houston peaked, and my mother faced some important decisions. We were scheduled to leave for Japan in late summer. Should she have us vaccinated against the disease at one of the many public centers, exposing us to large crowds and possibly polio? Or should she take a chance that we would not contract the disease? After the outbreak peaked, we were not allowed to go to the public swimming pool a few blocks from my grandparents' house and were sheltered from crowds of people. We were not vaccinated for polio, but we were fortunate not to be affected. Our cousin in Fairbanks, a Houston suburb, wasn't so lucky.

We each received a certificate like this after we crossed the International Dateline in the Pacific Ocean.

Good-bye, Texas; Hello, Japan

Shots, shots, and more shots. Every week Aunt Anna drove us to the Veterans' Hospital to get a series of shots—typhoid, tetanus, and cholera—that made us all sick. Frank and I were too young to have our own passports, so we had our pictures taken with my mother. Our destination was Nara, Japan. It would be a long trip: from Houston to San Francisco by train on the *Sunset Limited*, to Yokohama via a military sea transportation ship, and then to Tokyo by car. My mother wasn't sure if we would get to Nara by train or by car, but my father would be there to greet us when we disembarked. I wondered where we would live and what it would be like living in Japan. My father wrote to my mother that he had eaten octopus and squid. I wondered what we would eat. None of us had ever met any Japanese people, and now we were on our way to Nara, Japan. What lay ahead for us? It was August 1952. I was nine years old, and Frank was five.

During these preparations, life continued as usual in my grandparents' household. On Sundays their five children and thirteen grandchildren came for lunch. Usually my grandmother prepared one of her special meals, but one Sunday each month, my grandfather barbecued in his large smoker barbecue pit covered in bricks that he had made, and we sat outside in the backyard to eat. The round concrete table with three benches under the pecan trees could easily seat six to nine people. Frank and I helped put out the card tables and folding chairs. My mother helped in the kitchen, and I helped cover the tables with tablecloths and put out the silverware, plates, and napkins. My grandfather had also made several birdfeeders for the different kinds of birds that lived in the area, and kept the feeders filled with the appropriate seeds. My grandmother maintained the flowerbeds around the cyclone fence with lush evergreen plants, but the bed on the west side was always planted with colorful zinnias, which she could see from the kitchen window.

My grandmother played cards with several groups of women, comprised mostly of relatives, and frequently invited members of our large family for dinner during the week. My aunt took her to the store every Wednesday because she did not drive. My grandparents habitually woke early every morning and had breakfast together at 5:00 or 5:30. My grandfather still maintained his printing business with his younger brother and left for work shortly after breakfast. During the school year I walked to Horn Elementary and attended fourth grade in Miss Perkins' classroom. My mother walked Frank to a half-day kindergarten at the First United Methodist Church three mornings a week.

Our aunts and uncles or our cousins often invited Frank and me to spend the night with them, giving my mother a much-needed break. Sometimes my grandmother and I would ride the bus into downtown Houston and go shopping in Foley's. My grandmother always wore a hat with a veil, a suit, stockings, heels, and carried a matching purse. I wore a Sunday dress and good shoes. Before the outbreak of the polio epidemic, we swam in the neighborhood pool not far from my grandparents' house. The Popsicle man would drive down Jonathan Street midmorning and midafternoon during the summer. Sometimes we were given change to buy a Popsicle as a special treat. We played outside in our bare feet, and sometimes when my grandmother wanted to water the lawn, we put on our bathing suits and played in the sprinkler. In the evenings we watched television or played cards or board games. Once in a while one of our aunts and uncles would come by to see us. Sometimes we read books and colored, but life as we knew it was going to be different very soon.

We rose early on our departure day, dressed, and packed last-minute items. My grandmother prepared some of her special breakfast foods for us. We tried hard to eat and please her, but we were more anxious than hungry. After checking for any forgotten items, we loaded our suitcases into the trunk of Uncle Edward's car. My grandfather would drive from work and meet us at Union Station. Without the usual arguments about who got to sit by the window, we climbed into the back of the car like little soldiers. With a long last glance at my grandparents' house and yard, we rode silently to Union Station, my mother sitting between us and my grandmother in the front with Uncle Edward.

After the luggage was checked, we climbed into our compartment on the Pullman car of the *Sunset Limited* and organized our snacks, new coloring books, new crayons, and books. I glanced out the window and saw that most of our family had arrived to see us off. Great-aunts, uncles, and cousins were all there, and everyone appeared to be weeping quietly. We got off the train to give good-bye hugs. I felt a great sadness at leaving my family again, but I couldn't allow myself to show it because I had to take care of my brother and my mother. I was the oldest. What would happen to Frank and me if something happened to our mother while my father was away? Besides, with everyone crying so much, I began to think we would never return. This was surely the saddest day of my life.

My grandmother could hardly look at me. She opened her mouth to speak, but nothing came out. Only tears rolled down her cheeks as she held my head in her hands and kissed my forehead. My grandfather handed me a small bag of Baby Ruth bars, my favorite, while tears rolled down his cheeks, and then he hugged me closely. I kept wondering if we would ever come back, and if my grandparents would still be living if we did. I had never seen my mother so upset. I helped her by distracting Frank as we boarded the train again and settled in our compartment. With a trembling face, Frank sat close to my mother and began to whimper. I handed him a coloring book and some crayons. As we looked out of the window at our family, the engine revved. Suddenly, my mother's sister and brother-in-law appeared in the aisle by our compartment. We jumped up to say good-bye, and after a quick hug and kiss from both, the engine revved again, a whistle blew, and the *Sunset Limited* began to move out of Union Station.

At last we were on our way to Nara, Japan. As the train moved slowly out of the station, I thought my mother would never stop crying. I looked out the window at the family who had loved me so much and saw red faces streaked with tears. They ran after the train with faces stretched in pain, hands extended high, waving and grasping the air as if they were trying to catch time and hold it still.

Frank and I were glued to the windows, watching the changing landscape during the three-day trip to San Francisco. A porter came into our compartment every evening and pulled the beds down. We slept well at night while the train rocked back and forth. In the morning another porter knocked on our compartment door at the time my mother had requested. When we returned from breakfast, the beds had been made and pushed up into the walls of the compartment, making it a sitting room again. We went into the dining car for all of our meals. White tablecloths and heavy silverware covered every table. The waiters and the porters, who were all black men, were very kind to us. When we arrived in San Francisco, there was no one to greet us, but we took a taxi to our designated hotel and spent three days waiting to board the ship. Even though it was August, it was so cold my mother bought me a black wool jacket.

We arrived at the dock on the appropriate day and time and boarded the ship without incident. It did not take long to settle in our cabin, put a few things in the small closet, and return to the deck to watch our departure from San Francisco. The dock was crowded with civilians, dock workers, and military personnel, all watching as the ship slowly pulled away from the dock. Family members stood close to the edge of the dock, waving frantically to relatives on the ship, handkerchiefs pressed to their eyes. Passengers on board crowded the decks, waving, searching for loved ones on the dock, desperately hoping for one last look at a special loved one, tears clouding every eye. Watching the Golden Gate Bridge grow smaller as we headed out into the Pacific, I wondered if we would ever return to the States, and if I would ever see my grandparents, aunts, uncles, and cousins again.

Military sea transportation ships usually had board games like Scrabble, Parcheesi, Monopoly, and cards in the salon. This gave Frank and me an opportunity to meet other children, and it provided us with a safe place to be on the ship. Sometimes we were given permission to go to a friend's stateroom and play or just visit, but this was rare. My mother kept a very close watch on both of us.

Except for lifeboat drills, I thought this would be an uneventful trip. Get up, dress, eat breakfast, walk the decks until lunch. Eat lunch, rest, and read until supper, and then play games or cards until bedtime. After two weeks, we would be in Yokohama, my father would be there to meet us, and our trip would be over.

We had been at sea for about a week as the US naval ship cut through the smooth, quiet waters of the Pacific. We were standing in the main lobby after breakfast one day, and the ships' nurses were walking through groups of passengers applying Mercurochrome stripes on people's faces. I did not want any of it on me because I didn't know what it meant. We had already taken a battery of shots before we left Houston, and I certainly did not want any more. The nurses smiled as they worked their way through small groups of people standing randomly in the lobby. I stood close to my mother, and Frank stood on the other side of her, holding her hand. I asked her what they were doing, but she didn't know.

My mother was a very attractive woman and always dressed well. People were attracted to her warm personality and were willing to engage in conversation with her. She moved quietly among the passengers gathered in the lobby. I stayed where I was told to stay with Frank and anxiously watched her move, smiling and speaking with certain passengers. Although I was confident without my mother, I was unsure of this strange situation, and I wanted her to be with me. I was nine years old, but as the oldest child, I felt it was my responsibility to look after both my mother and my brother in my father's absence.

She returned with a smile and said, "We are crossing the International Date Line. We are supposed to wear our clothes inside out and backward or get swabbed with mercurochrome. This is to celebrate that we will have an additional twenty-four hours. In other words, we will have two days that are the same date."

"No!" I said angrily. "I don't want to wear my clothes inside out! I like this dress," I protested loudly, smoothing the front of my dress on my legs. "No!! I don't want anything on my face!"

"It's just for fun, Mary Lou. Look at those people over there," my mother pointed.

"No!" I repeated, watching a little boy across the lobby with tears rolling down his face. By this time a gray-headed nurse wearing a stiffly starched, gray and white uniform was staring down at me through lenses framed in thick white plastic. Her smile revealed teeth yellowed by time and food stains. Her weapon, the applicator of Mercurochrome, dangled in front of my face. Then suddenly the cold orange paint was slowly streaked on both of my hot cheeks.

I could feel the hard stares of everyone in the crowded lobby. I turned and ran, pushing open the heavy steel doors to the deck outside. I climbed and ran to the top of the ship as far as passengers were permitted. A cool breeze dried my tears. I was safe up there. No one could see my striped face or feel my humiliation. No one could possibly know that all I wanted was to be with my grandparents in Houston.

As more people appeared on the decks below, I grew lonely at the top. I decided to investigate the activity below, but first I had to find my mother. She was still on the deck near the salon. Frank was close beside her, wearing two orange stripes on each cheek. She was glad to see me and guided us to the main deck.

Soldiers were milling about, crowding the deck, but they were not in parade dress. Ties, hats, and medals were missing. No one stood at attention. In the middle of the deck was the largest tub I had ever seen. I could not imagine what purpose it would serve. I hoped it wasn't going to be a group bath. I had read that Japanese people went to bath-houses for a bath with other people, but we weren't in Japan yet. Sitting on a tall ladder inside the tub was a beautiful blonde-headed mermaid. Even her arms, supporting her position on the ladder, contributed to her overall beauty. I couldn't stop staring. The soldiers couldn't either.

In a few minutes, the soldiers were in a line in front of the huge tub. One by one they climbed a ladder attached to the side of the huge tub and walked out on a short diving board. They were presented to the mermaid and then, fully clothed, dunked in the tub. There were no tears from this group; each soldier climbed out of the tub, smiling and dripping wet. I forgot myself and started laughing with some of the passengers standing close by. It must have taken about an hour for each soldier on board to be initiated by the mermaid. It was the most fun we had experienced for some time.

The remainder of our ten-day sea journey was more relaxed. There were more people to talk to when we were out of our cabin, and passengers seemed to smile more often. The initiation of the soldiers and the nurses who applied Mercurochrome were the subject of endless conversations among the children. Our last day on board, the captain distributed official certificates from our ship, the USNS *General Sultan*, and the mythical ruler of the 180th meridian, saying that we had been found worthy to be "Trusty Golden Dragons . . . Duly initiated into the mysteries of the Far East."

1. My father, Frank, and me at Easter time outside our duplex in Kurokuriyama.
2. Frank, my friend, me, and my mother feeding the deer in Nara Park.
3. Frank and me in front of our Japanese house in downtown Nara. My mother is in the background.
4. Frank and me with toys our beloved Hatsie gave us, in front of the azalea bushes in the front yard of our Japanese house.

My Father, (left) Captain Carl Hughes, was commanding officer of the 79th Engineer Company in Camp Okubo, Japan. Lt. Wallace Uren was executive officer. This photo was taken November 18, 1954.

```
                        HEADQUARTERS
                  CAMP            NARA
                        APO 40



                                          22 December 1953



  Miss Mary Lou Hughes
  Quarters 113D
  Kurokamiyama Housing Area
  Camp Nara, Japan

  Dear Mary Lou:

  I am happy to be able to send you this photograph recording the
  presentation of Honorable Mention for your essay during Conservation
  Week.

  You have contributed materially to the success of the Army Savings
  Program by explaining how children can help reduce expenditures in
  the Far East Command.

  I thank you for your splendid spirit and excellent work.

                            Sincerely,


                            CONRAD B. STURGES
                            Colonel        Inf
                            Commanding
```

I was very proud of this recognition for an essay I wrote for "Conservation Week". The photo was lost.

Nara, Japan

Before we docked in Yokohama, my mother exchanged her American greenbacks for the colorful military scrip at the purser's window in the main lobby of the ship. It was much smaller than our greenbacks, and there were no coins, but the value of the paper money remained the same. Beautiful, pastel-color combinations on each denomination were an unusual characteristic of this money, and it was easy to feel the lines in the paper. My mother explained that using the scrip prevented too many US dollars from being circulated on the black market.

As we entered Yokohama Harbor, we watched from the deck, as American military personnel seemed to be giving orders to hundreds of small Japanese people moving hurriedly about on the dock. Ropes were thrown from the ship and slipped around thick, round pieces of metal jutting from the dock as the ship moved slowly into the slip. Despite the unusual, strong odor of the water, we stayed on deck searching the crowds on the dock below for my father while the gangplank was moved into place. Customs officers, medical personnel, and other military personnel boarded the ship first. In time, passengers disembarked in an orderly manner. My father was there to meet us and was especially happy to see my mother. He was a captain now, still in the Corps of Engineers, and commanding officer of the Seventy-Ninth Engineer Company at Camp Okubo, in Nara. When our luggage was accounted for, he supervised as the Japanese driver loaded all the suitcases into the army sedan. We climbed in the backseat with my mother; my father sat in the front with the driver. As we drove through Yokohama, we saw crowds of small-statured people with almond-shaped eyes and black hair, all going in different directions at the same time. In Tokyo hundreds of people were riding bicycles and many were pulling passengers in rickshaws. Still others were walking. There were people everywhere, and they were all moving. The traffic was congested nonetheless because the streets were so narrow.

The beautiful kimonos worn by Japanese women and girls were in color combinations I had never seen, bright pink and red for young girls with very elaborate brocade obis, which hold the kimono closed at the waist; muted colors for middle-aged women with more elaborate obis, and solid black kimonos for mature women with simple black obis. Supported by raised wooden platforms on the bottom of their feet, women and girls moved very gracefully. Even the men wore the wooden getas (wooden slides with thongs attached to two wooden supports). Women and girls wore zoris (ankle-high, tight-fitting socks worn with thong-type shoes) with their getas. I wondered how they could walk at all.

The men wore cone-shaped straw hats, happy coats (a shortened version of a kimono that covered the hips), and short pants with thongs on their feet as they pulled the rickshaws. The women who worked in the rice paddies wore cone-shaped hats too, but theirs were wider to protect their faces from the sun. They also wore dark blue or black happy coats, long black pants, and knee-high rubber boots so they could walk in high water. Some Japanese people wore Western-style clothing. Tiled roofs rested on small wood-framed houses, but as we left the city, the tiled roofs changed to thick thatch. In the city, houses and buildings were cramped together. There was no green space, but beautiful flowers and green plants grew from the most unexpected places. Every available piece of land was occupied by humans or farmed for rice. Even the hillsides and mountains were terraced in beautiful patterns for rice farming. My father informed us that the flowers were so large and beautiful because of the natural fertilizer used on all the plants. Human waste was collected and placed in small wooden buckets with a wire handle and a fitted wooden top called a honey bucket, then taken into the fields to fertilize plants. We recoiled in horror. My father assured us that the food we would be eating from the commissary was not fertilized from honey buckets. Furthermore, the army provided packets of something to sterilize any fresh fruits or vegetables we might purchase in the Japanese markets.

Our first night in Tokyo, the city seemed to be awake and moving well into the night. The sky was filled with colored lights. Traffic noise, horns, people walking on wooden getas and talking; it was never quiet. The language fascinated me, but even though I had studied some basic Japanese words and phrases while we were on the ship, I could not understand it at all. After being reunited with my father, driven from the port in Yokohama, and graciously shown to our hotel room, we began to relax from an exhausting day. As soon as we put down our suitcases, we had to wash our hands. We were told not to touch anything in the room, or walk barefooted on the carpet or the bathroom floor, because we were in a foreign country and could easily pick up unfamiliar diseases and germs. Washing our hands often was a habit we readily adopted, and one that we continued even after we returned to the States.

Luminous hands on the radio clock showed it was 3:30 a.m. I was almost asleep when I heard the sound of a human voice simultaneously screaming and singing coming from outside our fourth-floor window. I bolted upright in my bed, afraid that someone was just murdered. "What . . . was . . . that?" I asked. My father only laughed quietly and said it was the noodle man and to go back to sleep. Frank never moved in his bed. I wondered why anyone would want to sell or sing about noodles and who would buy them in the middle of the night. Later I learned that this was typical in Japanese cities. Maybe the noodle man was trying to earn extra money. Maybe that was his only job.

The next morning we left Tokyo in the army sedan and were driven to Camp Okuba in Nara. That evening we had a light supper at the mess hall, even though it was after hours, and then the driver delivered us to the old two-storied Japanese house where we would live.

It was late August 1952. I was nine and Frank was five when we walked through a thick wooden gate in a tall concrete wall surrounding the Kimoto property. Just inside the concrete wall near the gate sat a typical but smaller and newer Japanese house. My father, who was still wearing his green army uniform, said, "That's where Mr. and Mrs. Kimoto live. This is their property, but they are letting us rent half of the big house. Mr. Kimoto speaks English." Toward the back of the property was the large two-story Japanese house where we would live. At each corner of the roof, green tiles pointed toward the sky. On the second story, dark-brown wood created a European-style design in the white plaster-like surface of the walls. There were actually two identical houses connected by a long hallway. No other family lived in the second house while we were there. Dense fuchsia Formosa azaleas along the curving walkway concealed the front of the house and a screened front porch.

There were landscaped gardens with beautiful plants as well as tall pines and fruit trees. My mother walked behind my father on the narrow, curving concrete walkway leading to the large house. The Japanese driver unloaded our luggage from the army sedan and followed Frank and me to the front door. After neatly placing all the luggage inside the screened porch, my father thanked him and told him he was free to go. Using an old key in the front-door lock, my father opened the dark-brown front door as a strong, musty odor greeted us.

"No one has lived here for a long time," my mother said.

"We're the first people they've rented the house to," my father replied. "They'll send a crew out from the base tomorrow to hook up the electricity. These old houses are like matchboxes. The wiring isn't up to code, and it's not insulated well. As soon as somebody moves out, they always cut the electrical wires to prevent any fires."

Each of us picked up a suitcase and walked into the strange, old house with the musty smell. My parents ducked to pass through the low doorway. Light poured through the rice-paper screens covering the windows in the back of the house. Ivory-colored wallpaper with tiny light-pink flowers contrasted with the dark wainscoting. Sliding pocket doors covered with opaque rice paper gave a hint of privacy between the front room and rooms at the back of the house. We stepped on dark hardwood floors. Because of their height, my parents had to duck every time they passed through a doorway. Compared to my grandparents' house, the rooms were small, but the kitchen, which had glass-fronted cabinets with dishes in them, was nearly as large as my grandparents' two-bedroom house. There was a large drain in the middle of the floor. There were no closets or furniture in the house, just four army cots for sleeping.

I wanted to explore the upstairs, but my father firmly said no. "I want all of you to sleep downstairs. Upstairs, you'd never get out if this place burns. Mary Lou, Frank, you sleep in the room next to the kitchen. Sara, you and I will sleep in the room next to them." My father always talked to us like we were soldiers.

After a minute I said, "But there aren't doors to any of the rooms."

"You don't need doors to sleep," my father said.

"Well, where are we going to put our clothes?" I asked.

"Where can I put my socks?" Frank asked.

"Just leave your suitcase open and put them in your suitcase for now," my mother said.

"But if we get up to go to the bathroom we might step on our clothes in our suitcase," I said.

"We can push it under your cot after you take your bath," my mother answered.

"You and Frank go ahead and get out your pajamas now and get ready to take a bath. It's been a long day."

We followed her as she looked for and found the comfortably large blue bathroom with a long claw-footed bathtub, a sink, and a small commode that was not much higher than the tiled floor. We would have to squat to use it. My father stayed in the small room with the cots, looking over some papers he carried in his suitcase. A warm bath sounded good, but this wasn't like being at home or even in a hotel. *Would we have to live like this every day—without furniture and doors or curtains on the windows?* When we climbed into our cots, my father held a flashlight so we could see where we were going.

"My sheets aren't tucked in," I said.

"Mine don't cover me up," Frank said.

"The sheets aren't going to be tight like they are on your bed," my mother explained. "You can't twist and turn a lot. This is just for tonight and maybe tomorrow night. Then we'll have some beds." She unfolded Frank's sheet, covered him up, and kissed both of us. My father said, "Good night," as he followed my mother into the room next door, using the flashlight as a guide.

I wasn't sure I wanted to live here. The cot was very uncomfortable. There were no doors, no closets, and no lights. I whispered all of this loudly to Frank. "Yeah," he replied. "It's hot too."

"Quiet in there!" my father said.

The next morning it was hot and humid, but sunlight flooded through the rice-paper screens in front of the windows, making the house very bright. We ate cereal from a box that my mother brought with her. An army sedan waited outside the gate for my father. Later in the morning, a crew of Japanese men from the base came to reconnect the electricity. The house was low on the ground, and the spaces between the house and ground were covered with thick spider webs. Some even had dead bugs in them. Frank grinned at the sight of this, but it sent shivers through me. We watched closely as the three men, speaking fast in Japanese, wiggled under the house, moved through the dirt on their stomachs to the middle, and then reconnected the electricity. Their faces shortly reappeared at the edge of the old house, and they wiggled out from underneath, covered with spider webs and dirt. The men stood close together in front of us, smiling and bowing at us simultaneously, and then, speaking fast in Japanese, they headed for the gate.

Later in the day a three-quarter-ton army truck arrived in front of the gate and unloaded army-issued furniture. Now we all had a bed to sleep on in addition to some chairs, a table, some lamps, and two end tables. Frank and I spent the rest of the first day exploring the unusual plants and trees outside. We lived in a large house, but there were no closets or storage space, and my mother spent the day trying to find a place to put things.

When my father was at work and my mother was preoccupied, I went quietly upstairs and explored all the rooms. The wallpaper was the same as that on the living room walls, but built into the wall under each window was a large box with a sliding top. There was nothing inside, and I did not know what they were for, but much later in my life I discovered that the boxes were for storing kimonos.

While I explored the upstairs rooms, Frank searched the ground outside for live bugs and spiders. He must have been absorbed in his search for insects, not realizing where he was going, when he looked up and, through a small door, saw Mr. Kimoto sitting on a camp stool inside the concrete wall surrounding the Kimoto property. When Frank stepped inside, he startled Mr. Kimoto, who was wearing a painter's smock and painting with watercolors. The inside walls were finished with wood, and many of his watercolors, nature paintings, hung there. He had quite an array of paints and brushes to choose from. We were surprised to learn that the concrete wall surrounding the property was finished inside, and that it was large enough for a person to walk all the way around the property while inside the wall. We did not know that Mr. Kimoto was a painter. While we lived in the old house, Frank visited him several times when he was painting. He was always glad to see Frank and let him walk freely through the inside of the wall while he painted, but Frank never walked far out of Mr. Kimoto's sight while he was inside the wall.

That same week a young Japanese girl named Hatsue Imari came to our door. She was nervous and only spoke a few words in English, but she was going to work for us, and my mother was delighted to have her. Even though we only lived downstairs, it was a relief to have someone to help clean the large house. She was also company for my mother and for Frank, who was not old enough yet to go to school. We were her first employers.

She soon became like a member of our family, and at her request, we called her Hatsie. She was anxious to learn English, so I decided to help her with English lessons. Frank stood next to me, watching and listening closely as I exaggerated the shape of my mouth, rolled my Rs, and coaxed and oozed the sounds of long words out of my mouth. Frank repeated everything I said. Hatsie attempted to repeat the sounds I made. For emphasis, I put her hand on my throat so she could feel the vibrations in my vocal cords while I pronounced a long word very slowly. Then I put my hand on her throat to check for the same vibrations as she tried to pronounce a word, but my mother came into the kitchen just at that moment and must have noticed that Hatsie's eyes were very large. Quietly, she told me not to bother Hatsie while she was working. Furthermore, I was instructed never to put my hands on Hatsie's throat for any reason. Our English lessons continued when I thought my mother wasn't listening, but they were much less intense and less frequent.

When Hatsie finished her work, she would squat on the kitchen floor until my mother came in and asked her to do something else or let her go home early. She would never eat with us, and she always brought her own food from home. Squatting on the floor in a corner of the kitchen, she ate cold rice, fish, and vegetables from a bowl with chopsticks.

We had not lived in the old house long when my father walked toward the wooden gate at the front of the Kimoto property and told me to follow him. My father smiled when Frank said he wanted to come too. We were forbidden to be outside the gate unless an adult was with us, or unless I was walking to school.

Soon a large black limousine came by and stopped right in front of us. A small Japanese man dressed in a black suit was sitting in the back. He spoke English very well and conversed with my father for a few minutes before the driver handed me a soft brown puppy. I was delighted with this wiggly gift and handed it over to Frank. The puppy kept trying to lick and chew his fingers. The puppy's tail kept hitting his arms. Frank giggled and laughed and hugged his new friend, who was anxious to get down. We thanked the gentleman and the driver as they departed with very broad smiles.

We named our new friend Eppy and rushed inside to show our mother, who was not delighted with this active gift. Neither was Hatsie. Eppy lived in the kitchen for a while, but Hatsie complained when he made puddles on her clean floor, and soon he became an outside puppy. There was much for him to explore outside. Eppy became Frank's constant companion. They played together all day while I was in school, exploring the large property surrounding our house.

Sometimes, Harumi, a friend of Hatsie's, would come by to see her while she was working in the kitchen. They stood in the back door and chatted excitedly in Japanese, smiling a great deal. Harumi dressed in brightly colored Western-style clothing. The first time I saw her she was wearing a red suit and red high heels. Her shining black hair was cut in a medium-length page boy. Even her nails were polished in bright red. She never stopped smiling, and she was crazy about Frank from the first time she met him.

Hatsie asked my mother if she and Harumi could take me to see the geisha perform their annual musical in Kyoto on a Saturday. My father gave me some yen for myself and some extra to buy something for Hatsie and Harumi. Our ride to Kyoto on the bullet train was so smooth, it felt as if we weren't moving at all, but the landscape whizzed by us. When we entered or exited the coach, Hatsie stood on one side of me and Harumi stood on the other. The automatic doors slammed without warning. There was always a rush of pushing and shoving by people to enter or exit quickly.

In Kyoto we walked together, but I stopped to look at every shop window along the way, which irritated both Hatsie and Harumi because they did not want to be late. We arrived in a timely manner, and Hatsie bought our tickets for good seats midway to the front. Like the Kabuki theater, which is comprised of men only, this musical production was comprised of all one gender—women. During the performance, the actresses wore stunning kimonos. Other times they wore Western-style pants, jackets, and hats. Music was performed by an orchestra, but there was a musician playing the shamesan (a Japanese stringed musical instrument) as well. The women performed traditional Japanese-style dances and synchronized Western-style dances. The plot seemed to revolve around romance, happiness, and great disappointment.

It was hot and humid that day, and the theater did not have electric fans or air-conditioning. People in the audience used small hand fans to cool themselves. Hatsie and Harumi talked constantly unless the lights were dimmed. During the intermission, while my hostesses talked animatedly, I excused myself and went to the lobby to buy an ice-cream bar. When the performance was over, Hatsie and Harumi wiped their eyes like many of the other people around us. The audience, mostly women, applauded wildly as the actresses returned to the stage for a final bow, holding hands in front of the maroon velvet curtain.

After the two-hour performance, we slowly exited the theater among the crowds of people who had come for an afternoon of pleasure. It was still hot and humid outside as we looked for a place to eat. I was anxious to go inside any place to escape the heat and humidity, but we followed the crowd into the downtown area of Kyoto until we entered a small door to a restaurant. It took a while for my eyes to adjust to the darkness inside. Then I realized the walls of the restaurant were all black. It was so cool that I thought the restaurant was air-conditioned. It was a very nice, but very small, restaurant. Japanese women dressed in chic Western-style clothing were seated at small, round tables. No one was talking. The women glared hard at me and then at Hatsie and Harumi with disproving looks. They remained silent as we stood there in the cool, dark air, waiting to be seated. I realized quickly that it was not the difference in our height that created those hard looks. The women stared and frowned disapprovingly at me because I was an American. We were not approached by the attractive young waitress to have a seat. Hatsie and Harumi turned and left without saying a word. I followed them down the street in silence. On the next block we found a small cafeteria-style eatery, where we stood and ate our lunch in silence, surrounded by a crowd of diners who stood and talked nonstop.

As we made the long walk back to the train station, I could hardly stop staring at the silk or brocade kimonos worn by many Japanese women in Kyoto. I never could have imagined the color combinations or the beautiful patterns on them. I was equally intrigued by the landscapes, the old bridges, the streams, and the beautiful plants in unexpected places. Old concrete lanterns were everywhere I looked. To me, Kyoto appeared to be a magical place.

It was dark when we finally boarded the train and sat back comfortably in the stuffed chairs. Our car was full of passengers, but I found a seat across the aisle from Hatsie and Harumi. The train pulled away from the station and immediately picked up speed. Some Japanese men sitting in front of my hostesses and across the aisle from me were eating noodles in the accepted Japanese manner: scooping them up in a bowl with chopsticks, slurping and sucking them loudly into their mouths, chewing with gusto, and creating salivary noises that are appropriate in Japan. Hatsie and Harumi continued to talk quietly. I felt left out because I didn't have anyone to talk to, although I was happy to be sitting down and going home after a long day. On the way home I studied my program from the performance, and then I sang quietly to myself: *Sho sho jo gi, sho jo gi no ne wa wa, sung sung suni ata minadate, koi koi koi.*

Mama-san

After we had been in the old house for about a week, Mr. and Mrs. Kimoto and Mama-san waited outside by the front gate near their house to meet all of us one Saturday morning. As we approached our Japanese landlords, my father appeared stiff and did not smile. My mother looked frightened. Mr. Kimoto wore a suit, white shirt, and tie. Mrs. Kimoto wore black slacks and a black blouse. Mama-san wore a black kimono and obi. Both families stood and stared at each other for a long moment, and then Mr. Kimoto extended his hand to my father and introduced himself. My father extended his hand, and the two men smiled warmly at each other, exchanging names before introducing their families. My mother stood frozen in place. She did not move or smile until we went back inside the house. Frank stood close to my father. Mrs. Kimoto smiled at all of us, as did Mama-san. I smiled and nodded to each person; I couldn't wait to visit them.

About two months later, Mr. Kimoto invited my parents to dinner. Frank, who was five, and I, who had just turned ten, were not included. My father wore his dress blues, and my mother wore a very nice Sunday dress.

The next day my mother was excited as she told me about their evening. "We had Kobe beef with lots of vegetables that I didn't recognize and bowls of white rice. The food on each plate looked like a picture out of a magazine. We hesitated to touch it because we didn't want to ruin the 'picture,' but Mr. Kimoto told us it was all right to start eating."

"What did you drink?" I asked.

"We were offered Japanese plum wine when we sat down."

"That sounds awful!"

"It was very good, and we only drank a little bit. Mrs. Kimoto brought a pot of hot tea with four very small cups from the kitchen before she put the food on the table."

"What did the tea taste like?"

"It was clear and kind of bitter, but it was good to wash down the food."

"Where did Mama-san sit?"

"We didn't see her. Maybe she was in her room, but she never came out. Mrs. Kimoto must have been cooking all day, and Mr. Kimoto told us that they do not have a refrigerator. We sat on the *tatami* mats covering the floor and tried to eat with chopsticks. I think Daddy would like to have eaten with a fork because the food kept dropping from his chopsticks. We could only speak to Mr. Kimoto because Mrs. Kimoto doesn't speak English. The house is so small; I don't know how they walk around without bumping into each other."

When I look back now, I recognize the historic moment of that evening in Mr. and Mrs. Kimoto's home. Seven years earlier, the war started by Japan in the Pacific Rim had ended. My parents sat across from their Japanese landlords as friends, having dinner in their home while my father was wearing an American military dress uniform.

I asked my mother when she would invite the Kimoto family to dinner in our house. I was anxious to have Mama-san visit us, but when my mother said she didn't want to, I asked her why. She didn't give me a reason, and I was disappointed. I could tell that it was difficult for her to live in the old house. There were no other Americans in downtown Nara, and she did not have any friends or anyone to talk to. This made her anxious and a little jumpy sometimes. My father was preoccupied with his work, and I was in school. That left her at home with Frank and Hatsie. We were surrounded by well-established Japanese families who kept to themselves. When people passed us on the street, they looked right through us, or they looked the other way. It was as if we were not even living there, but in the late afternoons, sometimes the sound of classical Western piano music floated from the large two-story house next to the Kimoto property with regularity.

I did not realize that both of my parents might have harbored some fear while living in Nara seven years after the war. Perhaps they feared a reaction from Japanese people for political reasons. Maybe they were afraid of a reaction provoked by the sight of an American military uniform. If they did worry, they never shared any of those feelings with Frank and me, which freed us to meet and interact uninhibitedly with anyone Japanese.

One morning several weeks later, when Frank and I were playing outside, I looked up and saw Mama-san standing in the doorway of her room. She was smiling at me. When I returned the smile, she looked inside her room and then looked back at me, again smiling and nodding her head.

"Wait here," I told Frank. "I'm going to see what she wants."

"I'm gonna tell," he said.

"I'll be right back," I said and ran through the tall, leafy shrubs to Mama-san. She spoke quietly to me in Japanese and smiled so warmly. When I approached the sliding glass doors, she stepped back on the tatami mat and extended her arm inside the small room. I missed my grandparents very much. I was anxious to know this kind woman. I stepped up the three concrete stairs, removed my sandals, and put them on the top step before putting my bare feet on her tatami mat. Then I bowed low to her. She closed the door and gracefully sat down across from me. I glanced around the small white room quickly and noticed that it was void of any decoration. There was only the tatami mat on the floor. I was wearing wrinkled shorts and a sleeveless top that stuck to my body because of the humidity. She was wearing a long, black kimono with a simple black obi. Her hair was pulled back into a perfect, small bun at the nape of her neck.

She spoke in a quiet voice and never stopped smiling at me. She sat on her legs with her hands in her lap and her back very straight. I changed my position from sitting on my bottom to sitting on my legs like she did, but I couldn't keep my back straight for very long. I didn't understand a word she said, but I listened with rapt attention because I was so lonely. In a few minutes she touched the wall behind her. A small rectangular panel opened. She picked up a narrow black tray with two small, round black teacups, a small black teapot, and a very small dish with two cookies. The tea set made me think of a doll's tea set.

Without smiling she looked at me, her hands folded in her lap, and spoke for a minute. Then she poured the clear tea in each of the small cups. She placed the teapot carefully on the tray, placed her hands in her lap, and then smiled at me. I smiled in return and followed her every move. When she took a sip of tea, I did the same.

I was used to drinking Lipton iced tea with lots of sugar in a large glass with ice cubes. I took one sip of the hot tea in the small cup and carefully put it down on the tray. It had a terrible taste. It was mildly bitter, but she seemed to savor it. I looked into her black eyes and smiled. I didn't want her to know that I didn't care for this kind of tea. She continued to smile and talk quietly.

Whenever she picked up her cup, I did the same. When our cups were about half empty, she looked at the two cookies and smiled at me very warmly. I was hungry so I grabbed one, popped it into my mouth, and chewed vigorously. It was sweet and tasted like vanilla, one of my favorite flavors. Mama-san nearly dropped her tea. Her smile faded to a look of astonishment.

She placed her teacup on the small black tray, her hands in her lap, and smiled at me in a condescending way with her eyes lowered so she could only see the tatami mat. To my disappointment, she gracefully picked up the last cookie between her thumb and pointer finger and then took a small bite. I could not see her mouth moving at all when she chewed. Maybe the cookie was supposed to dissolve on the tongue, or maybe we were supposed to eat like birds. I waited and watched. She took a sip of tea before she placed the last bite to her lips, and then she placed her hands in her lap. I could barely see her chewing. I smiled to cover my intense embarrassment. She smiled very warmly at me in return.

Frank must have told my mother that I had gone into Mama-san's room, because I heard her calling me—and she did not sound happy. I excused myself to Mama-san, bowed low, and thanked her. I quickly put on my sandals, bowed low once again, closed the sliding glass door, and ran to find my mother, who had called me again, louder. As I walked through the tall green shrubs that separated our houses, I turned to look back at the small house and the sliding glass door one more time. Mama-san was standing in the doorway, smiling at me. I waved to her and she waved to me, and then I called to my mother that I was coming.

This was the beginning of a wonderful relationship. Many Saturday mornings, Mama-san waited in the doorway for me to come for tea. I loved being with her, listening to her talk, sharing the mildly bitter tasting tea. Most of all I loved her smiles. In time, I learned to sit on my legs with my back very straight and eat the delicious vanilla cookies like a bird.

One Saturday morning, I was having tea in Mama-san's room. She was speaking excitedly and louder than usual while her hands waved in the air, unlike her usual composed posture with her hands folded in her lap. Unexpectedly, Mr. Kimoto passed behind her, holding his Western-style shoes close to his chest, throwing a hostile look at her back, while his face became very red. He paused briefly; his eyes squinted with indignation, and his face was beet red. Then he turned quietly and passed through the small hall space. Mama-san was not aware that he was standing behind her or passing down the hallway, until I momentarily moved my eyes to his presence. When I looked back at her she was looking down at the tatami mat with a slight frown. Her hands were on the mat beside her instead of in her lap, one inside the other. It was then that I realized she expected me to pay attention to her whenever she was talking to me, which I did from then on.

I had not noticed that Mama-san's tiny room was missing a wall until Mr. Kimoto passed behind Mama-san that day. Perhaps she put a screen there at night for privacy. I did not know that Mr. Kimoto slept in the room next to Mama-san's room. I looked for a pause in her speech, excused myself, and rose to leave. I bowed very low, stepped into my shoes, bowed again, and slipped through the sliding glass door. I felt entirely out of place that morning. I was not sure if Mr. Kimoto was angry with Mama-san because she had woken him by speaking louder than usual, or if he was angry because she had invited me for tea. I waited several weeks before I returned on Saturday morning for tea.

Mama-san was a loving person, and having tea with her in her small room made me feel like the luckiest person in the world. She enjoyed my company as much as I enjoyed hers. When I looked across the tall green plants that separated our two yards and saw her standing in her doorway, she was always smiling at me. I knew that she wanted me to come to her room for tea and that she cared for me. If she had been my grandmother, I would have hugged her and kissed her every time I saw her; she made me feel that loved, but this was not the accepted Japanese way. Instead, I honored her presence with deep bows, and enjoyed the bitter tasting tea she made for me. I imitated her every move closely, and smiled as often as was appropriate. I didn't understand a word she said, but I listened with rapt attention.

Sometimes Mr. and Mrs. Kimoto invited Frank and me to come and have our picture taken with their friends on Saturday morning. They always gave my parents a copy of the picture. The friend set his camera up on a tripod while Frank and I stood in the shrubs separating the two properties, watching with interest. As the timer was set, we stood together closely, with Mr. and Mrs. Kimoto and their friends who did not have children. Mama-san never joined her family for pictures. The friends didn't speak English, and other than the word arigato (thank you), we didn't speak Japanese—but it was so much fun being in their pictures. It made us feel important, like we were part of a family again, and my mother especially loved the photos.

Mama san continued to wait for me to come for tea on Saturday mornings, but it wasn't long before Mr. Kimoto approached my father.

"Mary Lou, Mama-san wants to take you shopping with her this Saturday," my mother said.

"Really? How do you know?" I asked, surprised.

"Mr. Kimoto asked Daddy if it would be all right. You have to stay with Mama-san, and don't eat anything while you are in the market."

"I'm going to wear my pink dress with the little green umbrellas on it." My mother had made the simple short-sleeved dress out of silk pongee that she had bought on the Japanese market. It was my favorite dress. I loved the little green umbrellas and the silky feel of the pongee.

"That will be nice," she said.

"Okay," I said, smiling. I couldn't believe she was going to take me shopping, and I could hardly wait until Saturday morning. When the time came, my father reviewed the guidelines I was to follow one more time before I left.

"Do not leave Mama-san's side for any reason. Do not eat any food in the market. Be careful what you say. Do not speak to anyone that Mama-san doesn't speak to. Do you understand?" he bellowed. He always spoke loudly when he wanted to emphasize a point.

"Yes, sir," I answered.

"Here, this is for you to pay for the bus ride for you and Mama-san," he said as he took some yen coins out of his pocket. "I think Mama-san is waiting for you at the gate."

"Thank you, Daddy," I said, surprised at this unexpected gift.

"You look nice in your dress," my mother said as I left.

"Thank you." I smiled at her.

My father walked with me to the front gate, where Mr. and Mrs. Kimoto and Mama-san were waiting for me. Mama-san, wearing her black kimono and obi, was smiling broadly, and so was I. Mr. Kimoto and my father shook hands, spoke briefly, and watched as Mama-san and I moved out of the gate. Even wearing her getas, I was still taller than she was. I wondered how she could walk over the brick streets in wooden clogs without slipping, but I needn't have worried. She walked faster than I did in my sandals. I put my hand inside hers and held onto it as I would have done if she were my grandmother. After a moment of silence, she released my hand and spoke very quietly while she looked at the bricks in the street. Then she looked up at me and smiled warmly again as she put her hands together inside her kimono. I didn't touch her again.

As we walked to the bus stop, Mama-san continued smiling and talking in her quiet voice. It was only a few minutes before the city bus slowed to the same stop where the army bus picked me up for school every morning. We boarded the bus slowly, and I showed the driver some coins in my hand. He pointed to the correct fare which I dropped into the coin box, and we took our seats behind the driver. My presence was noticed on the street as we walked to the bus and then as we boarded. Some people stared, some concealed a smile, and still others looked away expressionless. I sat close to Mama-san, and she continued talking to me quietly. We didn't ride long before getting off the bus. I offered my hand to her as she descended the stairs. We walked from the bus stop into crowds of people walking to and from the market place. Many of the people I saw were wearing Western-style cotton clothing and thick, rubber-soled lace-up shoes, but about half the people passing us were wearing traditional Japanese kimonos, zoris, and getas like Mama-san.

The small stores displayed many of their wares outside on the sidewalk. I saw, exhibited up and down both sides of the street, everything a person would possibly need for a household. While I was looking around, Mama-san searched the goods in front of us. I picked up everything in sight, studied it, and put it back. Mama-san picked up a roll of toilet tissue and deftly dropped it into her kimono sleeve with a flick of her wrist. At the same time, she placed some coins in the hand of the shop owner with a smile and said, "Arigato." Mama-san and the shop owner chatted while I studied her long kimono sleeves for the shape of the tissue, but I couldn't find it. I was stumped. Where could she have put it? I tripped on the bricks while I walked around her, looking for the shape of the toilet tissue, and nearly fell. Mama-san chuckled, and the shopkeeper smiled. I kept staring at her sleeves waiting for the shape of the tissue to miraculously appear as she moved slowly toward the next shop. Lucky for me that staring is a polite behavior in Japan. I loved being with Mama-san in the Japanese market, and I stayed close to her as my father had instructed me to.

Mama-san took her time, letting me look at all the goods displayed in the open. After we left the market, we walked to a nearby street with small houses. She tapped lightly on a door in the middle of the block. An attractive young woman with short black hair and glasses opened the door. She was wearing a simple cotton dress that buttoned down the front and flat shoes with short white socks. We didn't go inside, but the young woman stood in the doorway talking to Mama-san and smiled often at me. I kept studying her kimono for the toilet tissue. I enjoyed being with the two women. It was like being with my grandmother and my aunt. After a short while I heard Mama-san say sayonara, and we started walking to the bus stop.

We waited for a short time with many other bus riders before the bus arrived and we took our turn boarding. I held out my hand with the coins my father had given me. The driver smiled as he took the coins to pay for our fare; Mama-san watched as he dropped them into the coin box. We headed for the middle of the bus while other passengers followed us down the aisle, looking for an empty seat. It was close to five o'clock, and the bus was crowded. We were quiet as the bus pulled away from the curb and headed back to our neighborhood. Mama-san seemed tired now. We got off the bus slowly and, following other people who walked down our street, made our way to the old wooden gate. She was slower now, but she nodded and smiled to those who acknowledged her. When we reached the gate, I pushed it open for her.

I turned and thanked her for the nice day, bowing low several times so she would know how much I appreciated her kindness. She looked at me and smiled, then bowed to me. I thanked her one more time, saying, "Arigato Gozimashita (thank you very much), Mama-san," bowed, and then headed up the curving concrete path to our house. I was glad to be home again. I loved being with Mama-san, but I had so much to tell my parents and Frank.

We continued to have tea on Saturday mornings, but several weeks later, Mr. Kimoto told my father that Mama-san wanted to take me to the citywide school sports competition in the large stadium outside of Nara. My parents were happy to let me go with her again. They loved my report of our shopping adventure in the Japanese market. My father gave me bus fare for Mama-san too. This time, Mama-san packed some lunch in a large cotton scarf. She tied the ends together and carried it like a purse. We retraced our steps to the bus stop and rode to the large sports stadium. It was about noon when we arrived and walked to the bleachers, where the competition had already begun. There were runners dressed in white shorts, shirts, and tennis shoes racing around the field, jumping over wooden saw horses. The crowd was riveted to the action on the field, but as we approached the bleachers to find a seat, I felt the stare of hundreds of pairs of eyes watching me closely.

I was the only Caucasian in the crowd, and at five feet tall, I was taller than everyone else. People in the bleachers stared hard at me. No one in our section was watching the field as we took our seats, which made me very nervous. Mama-san said something to me quietly and pointed to the field where the racing continued. I heard a whistle blow, and saw runners jump onto the track, running as fast as they could. After a while Mama-san pulled out a small bottled drink and offered it to me. I accepted gladly. Mama-san opened one for herself as well. Then she pulled out a red apple, rubbed it until it shined, and asked me if I wanted it. I accepted that too because I was always hungry, but when I bit into it rather loudly, pulling a large chunk of apple away from the fruit, Mama-san jumped, and everyone around me turned and stared, aghast. Mama-san pulled another apple out of her scarf bag, polished it, took a small quiet bite, chewed slowly, and swallowed. Then she turned and smiled at me. I understood. My next bite was only large enough to feed a bird.

Shortly, I had to use the bathroom. I asked Mama-san in Japanese where the bathroom was. She answered me slowly, and I repeated the directions to be sure I understood them correctly. She smiled at me with much affection. I excused myself and headed toward the gym and the bathroom. The students I passed along the way stared at me, their eyes large with wonder at my presence here at their competition. When I smiled at them, they looked down at the ground. I walked into the gym where two teams were playing an intense game with a ball and whistles were blowing. The bleachers were full, but the noise only came from the players on the floor. I followed Mama-san's directions and read the writing posted over the doorway leading down a long hall. I turned to the right and walked down another hallway. The writing over the doorway at the end read "Restroom."

A player from the field with an injury had been in before me. Bright red blood was running down the sink. The sight of it startled me as I entered the small room. I rinsed the sink thoroughly before using the low commode and washing my hands; then I found my way back to the stands. This time as I entered the bleachers where we were sitting, the people around us smiled at me. Mama-san smiled as I sat down. I told her in Japanese that I had found the restroom and thanked her for her directions. She spoke softly to me and smiled a lot. She reminded me of my grandmother so much. Mama-san seemed to tire easily, and it was hot. We left before the competition ended and did not get to see the awards ceremony.

I loved being with Mama-san and I enjoyed the day, but I didn't have anyone to talk to. My Japanese was very limited, and no one spoke English. The hard stares from people around us had made me wary and very nervous. We retraced our path to the bus stop and quietly rode the bus back our neighborhood. We walked slowly to the old gate at the Kimoto property. Before we parted I wanted to hug Mama-san and tell her that I loved her and thank her for the nice day, but instead I bowed very low several times and, in Japanese, thanked her for taking me with her. She stood still with her hands inside her kimono sleeves. She was breathing hard, but her eyes were shining. She was smiling as she bowed to me slowly and then stood very still for a moment. When she stood straight again, we both parted.

Japanese Life

The first week of school was difficult for me. I had to walk several long blocks from our house to the intersection of a main street. A military bus would stop and pick me up before heading to the top of Mount Kurokuriyama, where the American school was located. When I walked to the bus stop in the morning, there were no adults or children out walking. I was the only one on the wide brick street. No one else came and waited for the bus. I stood all alone on the sidewalk. In the distance I noticed large groups of uniformed Japanese schoolchildren on their way to school, staring at me while slowly crossing the street several blocks away. They paused on the sidewalk and stared at me a long time before moving on. They next day they crossed the street closer to the bus stop where I was standing alone, and they could have a better look at me. By the middle of the week they walked to the bus stop, where they stood and stared at me for a long time without smiling, or moving, or speaking—which terrified me. No one had ever stared at me in that way. My mother taught me that it was very rude to stare. I perceived them as suspicious and threatening. I looked for a place to hide, but there was no hope for an escape; in front of me were two empty lots across the street, and behind me was a row of locked gates and doors.

The students never took their eyes off me and never smiled, but the group moved toward me slowly until I was completely surrounded. I could not have escaped even if I had tried. Without showing any emotion and avoiding any eye contact, a group of students put their hands on me with great care, rubbing their hands back and forth on my arms, watching and feeling my skin. After touching me, the first group moved on, but behind them others took their place. Each student took a turn touching and rubbing my arms, but no one smiled, no one spoke, and no one looked at me directly. I was so terrified. I stood as still as a statue, staring at the ground while my heart nearly palpitated out of my chest. Finally, the last students moved on. I could not endure this every day. I wanted to run home and never leave the house. While I stood alone trying to decide whether to head home or go to school, the bus arrived. The door opened, and I ran up the stairs, sat down, and felt a rush of relief. I was too young and too frightened to know that people care for each other, even when they do not speak the same language. I realize now how kind and caring the students were to show their concern for me. They may also have been very curious about the American student. It was quite different with adults.

In the afternoon, the locks and thick chains that secured wooden gates to the houses on the street by the bus stop had been removed. If I looked through the narrow openings in the wooden fences just the right way, I could see small, but beautiful gardens in front of the houses. The quiet neighborhood I left in the morning was awake now and the sidewalks were crowded with people wearing kimonos and Western-style clothing hurrying to their destinations. There was also a lot of vehicular traffic in the wide brick street. As I exited the bus, I smiled at everyone, but people seemed to avoid my smile as well as avoiding me. It was as if I were not even on the street. I felt ignored, out of place, and that I shouldn't be in crowds of Japanese people. I crossed the street in front of the bus stop and walked down the wide brick street that led to the Kimoto property. I never saw any cars on our street and rarely saw any people when I was walking home, but when I did, I smiled and said, konichiwa (good afternoon). Sometimes a person might smile in response while looking straight ahead, but most of the time, it was as if I were not even on the street.

Each day more children would come to look at me and feel my skin. For several days this behavior continued. Finally, I refused to go to school. I explained what happened in great detail, but my mother only said, "I'm sorry, but you have to go to school no matter what. Why don't you just try smiling?"

The next day as I stood waiting for the bus, a crowd of Japanese students approached me. Holding my head down, I stood as still as I did every day. They approached and surrounded me closely, but I looked up with a big smile, and I bowed very low.

As I stood smiling and bowing, they applauded, smiled, and bowed low too. There was happy chatter among them. From that day on, I received many smiles as I waited for the bus. Every day for at least a week, I smiled and bowed very low when I saw them approaching me. From then on, I waved and smiled whenever I saw them passing by me on their way to school. They smiled and waved back to me. We could have been friends if we had spoken to each other in the same language. My father later explained that no one in Nara had seen American children yet, and the Japanese students were probably just as curious about me as I was about them. From this experience, I also learned that in Japan it is very polite to stare, a habit I readily adopted because there was so much to absorb in this culture that was so different from my own. When we returned to the States, I was frequently reminded not to stare at people.

Sometimes when my parents took us to visit Japanese attractions, we noticed that some Japanese people gave us disapproving looks. Conversely, a Japanese person might step in front of us and bow deeply. My father was careful to guide us away from anyone who displayed strong emotions. Sometimes an adult passing me on the street would bow low to me while I waited for the school bus, which embarrassed me to death, although I was careful to return the bow. My mother explained that it was because we had conquered the Japanese during the war.

"But, Mother, we don't even know these people," I exclaimed.

"No, we don't," she answered, "but that is their way of honoring a conquering people."

No one had ever honored me or my family with a deep bow before. When that occurred, I felt so out of place and very embarrassed.

Meanwhile there was so much to discover in the old house. When Frank and I were playing in the living room one day, we found that a small square in the wall moved when we touched it lightly. To our surprise, there was a crawl space connecting two rooms. We could not imagine why there would be a crawl space hidden in the living room wall. It was lined with the same wallpaper as the living room walls. We took turns sticking our heads in the opening, trying to see where it ended, when I realized that Frank could fit nicely into the space. I convinced him to crawl into the space and hide while I closed the opening. I opened it again to make sure it would still work. Then I went into the kitchen to find my mother.

"Mother," I said calmly, "Frank disappeared."

"What do you mean, he disappeared?" she said, turning to look at me in alarm.

"Well, we were in the living room, and I touched the wall by accident. It moved, and then Frank crawled in and it closed. I looked everywhere for him, but I can't find him."

She burst into tears and started running to the living room. Now I knew I had made a mistake. I followed closely behind her into the living room.

"Where is he?" she cried loudly. "Where is he?"

I walked quickly to the wall with the moving panel and touched it. The smiling face of a five-year-old looked up at her while resting on his hands and knees. She angrily admonished me never to do that again. Furthermore, Frank was never to crawl into that space again. We never did, but we exchanged smiles as she left the room.

One Saturday morning when the weather was nice and cool, I went to Mama-san's room for tea. She wanted the sliding glass door left partially open that day. We had not been sitting too long when I heard her say, "No," in perfect English. Hearing her speak a word of English startled me; I thought I had stared at the cookies on the tea tray too long. But when my eyes moved from Mama-san's face to the tray, I saw that Eppy was about to take a cookie in his long pink tongue. His tail wagged vigorously, and his small brown-and-white body quivered at the sight and smell of this newfound delight. I grabbed the puppy, apologized, bowed, and left Mama-san sitting on the tatami mat in dismay. Her small, narrow eyes looked down at the tea tray. Her long, bony fingers were splayed on the straw mat, not folded formally in her lap, as I was used to seeing them.

It wasn't long before Eppy entered Mr. and Mrs. Kimoto's house uninvited and chewed some of their tatami mats. After this incident, Mr. Kimoto approached my father about the dog. From then on, Eppy was tied to a fruit tree behind the kitchen. This arrangement pleased both my mother and Hatsie.

Although my parents discouraged Frank from going near the Kimoto house, he loved exploring the grounds around both houses. One day he happened to be outside when he saw three men raking up leaves and branches; the branches had been cut from some of the trees hanging over the concrete wall. While Mama-san observed, the men brought leaves and branches from outside the concrete wall, broke all the branches into smaller pieces, and raked the debris into a neat pile, and then Mama-san struck a long match and threw it into the pile. Frank was alarmed at the sight of fire and smoke. He ran toward the debris, kicking and scattering the leaves and branches. Mama-san and the men stood in wonder at this behavior but did nothing to discourage Frank. The men raked the debris into a neat pile once again. Mama-san lit another match and threw it into the leaves. Now Frank was really alarmed and ran toward the pile of leaves, kicking and scattering leaves and broken branches more forcefully. This time Mama-san spoke to him quietly in Japanese and pointed at our house, discouraging him from coming near the pile of leaves and branches. This only made the five-year-old boy more determined to put out the fire, because our father had stated so emphatically how dangerous fire could be to us, how quickly our house could burn, and how many times people could not get out of their houses when fire started.

Despite the miscommunication, Mama-san and the men tried a third time to burn the leaves and branches, but to no avail. Frank, afraid they were trying to burn their house and ours too, scattered the neat pile of broken branches and leaves all over the Kimoto yard, stepping on anything that smoked or burned. When it appeared that the men would not try to resurrect the debris and Mama-san would not light another match, he went to our house and reported his actions to our mother. Later on, Mr. Kimoto explained to my father the purpose of burning the leaves and broken branches. Mama-san was going to bury a piece of meat in the burning debris to cook for their supper. He asked that Frank not be allowed to interrupt when that action occurred. My father explained this to Frank, and he understood—but he never saw the men gathering leaves and branches again, nor did he see Mama-san lighting a match to burn the leaves.

Hatsie was a quiet, gentle presence in our home, and we looked forward to her arrival every morning. Because she was the oldest of six children, my mother often gave her clothing we had outgrown or could no longer use. Every gift was welcomed by her family. Sometimes, when my father was not home in the evening, she would prepare a Japanese dish for our supper, which was always a treat, but she would never eat with us.

Hatsie was more like a big sister to me than a maid, and my parents let me go everywhere with her. One day she took me to meet her family. We walked to the bus stop and rode a long way across Nara. When we got off, we were in the middle of a bustling commercial street of small stores. Each business had goods placed in front and along the sidewalks, making it necessary to walk in the uneven cobblestone street. We entered a dark, narrow alley almost hidden by a display of goods. After walking a short distance, we entered a small doorway, removed our shoes, put on zoris, and climbed steep, narrow stairs to the top floor.

The small living space was flooded with natural light from small windows close to the ceiling. Tatami mats covered the floor. The room was void of any decoration that I could see and was absolutely spotless. Smiling faces appeared from behind a sliding rice-paper door. Wearing glasses, a simple blouse, and a skirt, Hatsie's mother was the first to greet me, followed by her five younger brothers and sisters. One of her younger brothers also wore glasses. They appeared to stair-step in height and were all dressed in neat, Western-style clothing. We sat on the tatami mats with our legs folded under us. Hatsie offered me some orange drink in a clear glass. I noticed that one of her brothers had a newspaper under his arm, and I asked to see it. Hatsie didn't make a sound but glanced at her brother, and in a flash the paper was in front of me. I withdrew from the silent audience staring at me and spent more time than would be considered polite looking for any Japanese letters and words that I might recognize from my Japanese studies.

Hatsie called my name and again offered me a glass of orange drink, which I found much too sweet. The mantra my father taught us appeared to solve my dilemma. "Smile, eat the food, and don't say anything." I sipped almost half of the drink while politely answering questions posed by Hatsie's siblings, which she translated. They each had a question for me. They were interested in our feelings about Japan, and they also wanted to know if I missed living in Texas. They were especially interested in details about our family gatherings when my aunts, uncles, and cousins gathered at my grandparents' house. Our visit was shortened by long afternoon shadows darkening the room. I bowed and said sayonara to each of her brothers and sisters, who smiled warmly as they bowed and said sayonara to me. Hatsie and I headed down the narrow staircase, put on our shoes, and walked out into the alley again. We sat quietly on the bus and exited into early evening darkness on the other side of Nara.

Several weeks after my visit to Hatsie's home, she arrived earlier than usual smiling broadly and carrying a large box tied with a beautiful ribbon. She handed it to me and said, "Happy birthday, Mary-san." I was so surprised I couldn't say anything but a quiet "thank you." I hurriedly untied the ribbon and carefully opened the special paper while my mother watched. Inside the box was a beautiful cotton kimono and obi that Hatsie's mother had made for me. The white fabric had large maroon flowers with blue centers. It was completely lined with a thin white fabric and fit perfectly. The sleeves were long, which was appropriate for my age, but did not reach the floor. The hem was just the right length. My mother announced that it was a work of art.

"Look at the stitches," she said. "This was made this by hand, and it fits you perfectly through the shoulders." Hatsie blushed with pleasure at our excitement. My mother was very moved by this loving gift from Hatsie's mother, who had only observed me for a short time while I sat with my legs folded under me. It was more than a gift to me. It was a treasure that I still have. I wore it often with great pride.

Periodically, my father was officer of the day and was required to spend the night on the base. In October 1952, we were still living in the old house, and it was his turn to stay overnight on the base. That night a typhoon hit Nara. The wind blowing through the creaking old Japanese house agitated my mother. Even though it was dark outside, Hatsie was still with us. I suggested we all sit at the dining-room table and play a game. The winds began to pick up, and soon our phone line went down. I suggested that Hatsie spend the night with us. My mother agreed that she should stay over, but in order for us to do so she had to let her family know.

Although she had to go out in the bad weather to find a phone, Hatsie was anxious to spend the night. My mother became more agitated at the thought of her going out in the dark with high winds and drenching rain. Frank and I found a flashlight. My mother gave her a plastic raincoat that was much too big and an umbrella. We watched her open the screen door and walk out into the pouring rain and strong winds. We stood on the screen porch watching her until she closed the old wooden gate. For about fifteen or twenty minutes, we sat at the table in silence, worrying about her until we heard the screen door open, signaling Hatsie's return. She was relieved not to have to wait for a bus to take her across Nara and then walk to her parents' home. Eventually, the electricity went out too, but Frank and I had put some candles and matches on the table, so we were not in total darkness. The stormy weather, the creaking Japanese house, and my father's absence all made my mother especially anxious that night.

After we moved to Kurokuriyama, the American compound, Hatsie continued to take me places. Our visit to a Shinto shrine, built before nails were used in construction, was a memorable one for me. Hatsie did not want to go inside, but I spoke to the beautiful priestess, saying, konichiwa (Good afternoon) with a smile and a low bow. She responded to me in the same way, but did not smile. Her face was covered with the white makeup worn by geishas. On top of her head there was a small brocade hat shaped like a bird's beak, but the beak was worn backward, facing behind her. A thin piece of gold elastic held the hat on her head. Her thick black hair was straight and cut bluntly underneath her ears. She wore a long red robe edged in gold brocade, and matching getas. As I stood looking at her, she appeared very nervous, constantly opening and closing a white fan that she held in her hands. I never understood why my presence made the priestess so nervous. Hatsie did not elaborate about her behavior.

The priestess stood by a long, narrow red table in front of the shrine. It was covered with small, beautiful brocade pockets, each with a paper inside. They were in different colors, and each had a matching frog closure. I picked up several, admiring the beautiful fabric and interesting shapes. I asked Hatsie if I could have one, and she said yes. The priestess, who was observing me closely, frowned and shook her head no, forcefully. I returned the "pockets" to the table but held on to one made of green brocade with a gold-colored frog. I looked at Hatsie again. She glared angrily at the priestess, held her hands together tightly, and said loudly, "Yes!" I offered to leave some yen with the priestess, but Hatsie shook her head no, forcefully. We walked away quietly, while the priestess stared at the ground.

The Old House

It was difficult for my mother to live in the old Japanese house because she was alone so much. Although Frank was home with her and Hatsie came every week day, she was quite isolated. When housing on Mount Kurokuriyama, the American compound, became available, my parents were anxious to move again. I wouldn't have to ride the bus to school every day, Frank would have children to play with, and my mother would have American women to talk to. I loved being close to Mama-san, I loved the old house, I loved the plants and trees in the gardens. It was peaceful there, but while I was at school a crew from the base came to the house and packed up all of our furniture, dishes, suitcases, clothing, our books, and moved it to the American compound on Mount Kurokuriyama.

When school ended on that moving day, I walked to our duplex, which was located in a cul-de-sac not far from the guarded entrance of the compound. Luckily, we were on the end of the building and only had neighbors on one side. Eppy, our dog, was chained to the persimmon tree on the side of the duplex. His doghouse was placed close to the tree.

As I walked through the front door and entered the living room, I could see that the living space was much smaller than the downstairs living space in the old house. There was a lamp on each end table, there were a few ornaments on the bookcase, and ashtrays were everywhere. The furniture had already been arranged the way my mother liked it. The dining-room table was in the area off the small kitchen. With help from Hatsie, all the drawers and shelves had been lined with shelf paper. My mother already had the kitchen things put away. Hatsie had cleaned the bathroom, the kitchen floor, and vacuumed the living-room rug. Our clothes hung in the bedroom closets. Hatsie looked tired, as did my mother, but they were both smiling.

Frank and I shared a bedroom, and there was only one bathroom, but there were closets and hardwood floors. The kitchen, on the east side of the duplex, faced a tall cyclone fence with lots of rolled barbed wire on top. On the other side of the fence was a thick forest. There was no yard in the back, and the ground sloped in a downward direction past the fence to the trees, which grew in a sloping downward diagonal. We were literally on top of the mountain.

When I asked my mother if she and my father had said good-bye to Mr. and Mrs. Kimoto and Mama-san, she said no, they didn't have time. The truck had to be back on the base by two o'clock. I could not believe they did not stop and speak to these wonderful Japanese people who had been so kind to us while we lived in their old two-storied house. What would Mr. and Mrs. Kimoto think? What would Mama-san think of us? She was so kind. She was like a grandmother to me. I loved her so much. I wanted to cry. I went to my new room. I hated the room, and I hated sharing it with Frank. We even had to share the closet. I hated that too. I took the bed closest to the window that looked out on the paved cul-de-sac and the duplexes across the street. Only a few azalea bushes had been planted underneath the window. Otherwise the small front yards were covered in grass and green weeds. Mama-san! Mama-san! I had to find a way to see her again.

After we had lived in the duplex for about a month, my mother asked me one morning if I had any money hidden away. When I asked her why she wanted to know, she said the military was changing our monetary scrip because too much of it was on the black market. It would be worthless if I didn't give it to her to exchange. The only hidden money I had consisted of my allowance, twenty-five cents a week, and babysitting money. Most of the time I spent my money on Snickers bars or bubblegum at the small PX (post exchange) in the compound.

There was no other place and no other way to for me to spend any American money. I kept all of my money in a little wooden box with sliding sides and a small pull drawer that made a funny noise when it opened—a perfect place to hide money. I kept the wooden box with letters from my grandmother in a shoe box in the closet. I wondered what the new scrip would look like. My mother assured me that we would not be using greenbacks. It turned out that the new scrip was smooth to the touch—as were greenbacks—and the colors were not as brilliant as the scrip that had been issued to us when we had arrived in Yokohama.

I missed walking to the bus stop on school mornings. I missed seeing the empty lot across the street from the bus stop, where pine trees and a number of large rocks were placed throughout the lot. A low rock wall with a small piece of chain between each of the low rock posts surrounded the entire lot. It could have been a park, but there were no benches or walking paths. I never saw anyone walking through the empty lot. A morning wind rustled the trees, and the birds were usually singing in the mornings. Roof tiles on the houses behind the bus stop curved up gracefully at each corner. The houses, which opened right onto the sidewalk, were gated and always locked when I arrived, but the muted colors of dark red, shades of brown, and natural wood created a tranquil environment with the empty lot across the wide, bricked street.

Although there were children in my class who lived on our street in the compound, I continued to walk to and from school by myself. Our school population was small, and there were three grades in each classroom. I was friends with everyone, but I mainly kept to myself. Several months later, I asked my school friends Betsy and Billy, whom I played with at recess, if I could spend the night with them on a Friday night. They lived in a small house in downtown Nara. They rode to and from school every day with their father, but sometimes they rode the army bus home from school in the afternoon. Our parents knew each other because the American military community was small. I was ecstatic when my mother said I could stay overnight with them. If I could spend the night at their house, I knew I could find a way to see Mama-san.

After school, we boarded the army bus I used to ride. When I got off the bus, I wanted to run down the street to our old house and the Kimoto property, but I controlled myself and followed Betsy and Billy to their house. It was much smaller than our old two-storied house. Mrs. Gardner was glad to see me, but I wanted to walk to the Kimoto property before it got too late; I had to see Mama-san. I asked if we could walk to the old house where I used to live, and she agreed to let Betsy and Billy go with me.

We turned the corner to our former street and headed for the old wooden gate. I crossed my fingers on both hands and hoped that Mama-san would be home. I tried to hide my excitement, my anxiety about this visit. What if she isn't home, I wondered. What if someone else is living in the Kimoto house now? What if the gate is locked? Betsy and Billy kept walking slower and slower. They kept saying the Japanese were mean people and asking why I wanted to go see this old Japanese lady. I walked a little faster every time they asked me something and talked about school instead as we approached the gate.

I pushed the gate open, and my eyes flooded with tears at the sight of the old house, the Kimoto house, and the gardens. My heart pounded with joy while Betsy and Billy stood behind me, asking, "Who lives in this crappy house anyway?" I walked up the curving path toward our old house to get away from them, and then I turned to face Mama-san's room and called her name loudly, knowing it was not the appropriate or accepted Japanese way.

"Mama-san! Mama-san!" I shouted. There was no sign of life anywhere. I called again, louder, "Ma-ma-san! Ma-ma-san!" I waited and stared at the sliding glass door for some sign of life when Betsy said, "Look we really need to go now. This place is creepy."

"She's coming! Look! There she is!" I said, beside myself with excitement. Through the glass door I could see her frail body roll over on her futon, stand up while steadying herself on the wall, moving at a snail's pace, trying to slide the glass door open.

"I'm ready to go," said Billy.

"She's coming now," I said.

"I don't care," he said.

I knew it would not be good for a young American girl to be out on the street alone, even in the late afternoon. I had to delay Betsy and Billy from leaving. The threat of being left alone frightened me, and I became aggressive in my behavior, rushing ahead, calling loudly, "Mama-san!" and hugging her, which was not appropriate for any Japanese, and certainly not an elder. She said only my name, plucked an azalea blossom from the bush beside her, and placed it behind my right ear, stroking my head. "Ma—ry-san," she said quietly. I was speechless. Tears washed over my eyes as she stood looking at me. She coughed a little, placed her hand over her mouth, and coughed again. A small trickle of blood appeared in the corner of her mouth. Our eyes locked.

Betsy stood close by and gave me a knowing look, announcing loudly, "She has tuberculosis." She moved away from me and stared in disbelief.

I took a tissue out of my skirt pocket and wiped the spittle from the corner of her mouth. Gently, I embraced her again and stood looking at her frail body. Tears spilled from my eyes as she stood still and looked at me lovingly.

Betsy and Billy moved toward the old gate. "Hey, let's go before we all get TB," Billy said loudly. Betsy looked indignant. How could I have brought them to this place? Her hand was on the gate handle. I looked at them and wished they would just leave so I could stay here with Mama-san. They glared at me and pushed on the gate while Mama-san stood watching.

I looked at Mama-san and whispered, "Sayonara, Mama-san, sayonara." Her eyes crinkled when she smiled. "Ma—ry-san," she said quietly in a gravelly voice. Billy struggled as he pulled the heavy, old gate open. I looked down at my feet to hide my tears and walked slowly toward the gate. Betsy was standing in the street with her hand on her hip, frowning at me. Billy stood next to her with his hands in his pockets, scuffing his tennis shoes on the bricks in the street. I stood in the gateway, turned for one last look at Mama-san, and waved. She stood regally with her head held high, her hands in her kimono sleeves. She nodded to me as I shut the gate quietly and turned to Betsy and Billy who were moving slowly up the street.

Walking fast, I caught up with them, but didn't say anything. Barb turned and looked directly in my eyes, "You need to wash your hands as soon as you get inside our house!"

"That old lady gives people TB!" Billy said loudly. "She's a carrier!"

"I certainly hope we don't get it," Betsy said.

The Park, the Temples, and Nara

While we were living in the old Japanese house, we went to the Officer's Club for Sunday lunch several times. It was located in an old building on the base in downtown Nara. Once, I was allowed to take my friend from school, Sue Ellen, as my guest. After lunch, we walked to the park and fed the deer, which were tame. They walked close to us, and let us pet them. Frank especially enjoyed the deer. Sue Ellen and I took turns petting those that came close to us. We loved the large koi fish swimming in the pond too. Several kimono-clad women wore long, dark-blue aprons with fish food in the pockets that they sold to park visitors. They always clapped when the fish jumped up for a food treat. Japanese families in the park seemed delighted to watch us enjoy a treasured Japanese pastime. Some people, however, were offended at the sight of my father's uniform. It was not unusual to see a few young men staggering across the park, drunk from *sake*, rice wine. My parents attributed this to their acceptance of the American presence in Nara, especially when they stopped and studied us before they wobbled past.

In the fall, we walked to the park and watched the ceremonial cutting of the deer horns. The center of the park was marked with wooden sticks and red ribbon where the deer were contained. Master cutters wore elegant happy coats and headbands of bright red ribbon. One at a time, the deer were taken from the temporary enclosure and presented to the cutters. The head was held firmly in place by two men, one on either side, while the cutter sawed the horns off. The deer did not struggle or appear to be hurt when they were released. A large stack of horns lay near the enclosure with the deer.

While we lived in the old house, my parents took us to see the enormous Buddha in To dai-ji Temple. Inside the altar where the Buddha was situated was richly decorated. Burning incense produced a sweet, musty odor, which I enjoyed. Enormous round pillars supported the ceiling. One of them had a small opening at the bottom. It was said that anyone who could crawl through it would have lifelong luck. I was encouraged to try it and with a lot of wiggling, making myself thin, and holding my breath, I managed to get through the small hole in the thick column. I wiggled out thinking I was going to be lucky for the rest of my life. Although my parents encouraged Frank to wiggle through as well, he wasn't interested.

A quiet stillness unified the Japanese people who paid their respects to Buddha and the tourists who gaped in wonder at the presence of the enormous black statue. Later, my father took Frank and me to see another Buddha, equally enormous, the Daibutsu, outside on the mountaintop not far from our old house. Part of this exhibit included a huge gong that rang when it was struck with a long, thick tree trunk encased in wide leather straps hanging from a sturdy wooden frame. Sometimes we heard the gong ringing from our house in downtown Nara; only a person of great strength could ring the massive gong.

Wind whispered through the tall trees on the mountaintop as Japanese families walked quietly and orderly around the grounds, paying homage to their deity. The simplicity of the black stone statue was one characteristic of its beauty. There was a peace and tranquility present that I had never experienced. All of this struck me as a gift to a higher being.

My father paid the small fee and took his turn to try and ring the gong. He did ring it, not once but many times due to his extraordinary strength. Japanese eyes grew large with astonishment as they turned to see who was strong enough to keep the huge gong ringing. My father chuckled as he reached up to halt the movement of the long, thick log and the peaceful silence resumed. Chattering Japanese surrounded us. My father enjoyed the awed looks of the workers and visitors as we walked away from the gong. When we returned to the old house, my mother confirmed that she had heard the gong ringing rapidly several times. This pleased my father very much.

Our first year in Japan brought many changes to my life, not the least of which was the infusion of Japanese culture that I loved so much. In Nara, May 1 was cause for a different kind of celebration than those we celebrated at home. It was the Communists' celebration and something everyone feared because of rioting and looting. Shops were closed. There was no traffic to and from the base in downtown Nara. There was no bus service from Mount Kurokuriyama to the base. None of the Japanese who worked as maids, clerks, secretaries, custodians, groundskeepers, maintenance men, or in any capacity for the Americans worked that day. Everyone, including the Japanese, stayed home behind locked doors. My father was required to stay overnight on the base. The Japanese security guards at the entrance to Mount Kurokuriyama were doubled on May Day, but my mother was still frightened.

When my father came home from the base on May 2, he reported break ins, looting, sake bottles, and litter strewn during the parade, as well as arrests made. When I asked my mother why this day was so special to the Communists, she said they wanted to take the government away from Emporer Hirohito and they did not like Americans being in Nara. Not long after this she told me not to tell people that my father was in the military.

"If anyone asks you what your father does, just tell them your father is in the service and don't say anything else."

"Why?" I asked

"Just don't," she said. "They might not understand why we are here."

During our first summer in Nara, my mother took me downtown to buy a bathing suit because she wanted me to take swimming lessons at the pool on the base. Frank went with us. We rode the bus into the downtown shopping district and walked the narrow brick streets, looking in the windows for young girl's clothing. Most of the stores appeared to be the front of the store owners' homes. In one instance, we walked down a curving street and when I turned my head to the right, I noticed two young boys wearing bathing trunks having a sword fight in the display window. "Oh, look, those boys are having a sword fight!" I said to my mother. She stopped to look. Frank thought we were going in so he could play too, but the mother of the two boys came rushing into the window and shooed the boys away. She smiled gracefully to my mother while bowing to all of us. We smiled and bowed to her and then continued walking.

A little farther down the street, my mother noticed a girls' bathing suit displayed in a window with other children's clothing. It was not on a model as we would see in the States but placed on the floor of the display window. We went inside the small shop and with some pointing my mother indicated she was interested in the dark-blue bathing suit for me. The Japanese lady inside, anxious to please my mother, talked excitedly, bowed repeatedly, and smiled from ear to ear. She found a bathing suit that might fit me in a drawer filled with socks and underwear. My mother held it up to me to check the size, but the lady insisted that I try it on. Even though my mother said it was all right, I was embarrassed to do so. I was afraid young boys would come and take a peek while I was changing, but no one did. I stood behind a shower curtain in a small changing area that seemed like a closet. I tried it on and then called to my mother. She liked the way it fit me, and I liked it too. I was nervous about changing my clothes in a stranger's home and took longer than usual. The Japanese lady was so pleased that the American lady with two children had come into her shop to buy something. She couldn't stop smiling or talking or bowing. My mother was also pleased.

The bathing suit served me well. I took diving and swimming lessons that summer. My mother, Frank, and I rode the bus from Mount Kurokuriyama every weekday morning to the base in downtown Nara. While I was in the deep end of the pool with about eight other children, my mother watched Frank play in the wading pool with children his age. The mothers visited with each other while we were swimming. When the lesson was over, we rode the bus home, had lunch, and lay down for a nap.

Once I found myself in downtown Nara with Mama-san in the early morning. We walked slowly because Mama-san was not in a hurry that day. I didn't want to miss anything while we were shopping, and my eyes roamed the streets. Uniformed children were walking to school with small portfolios tucked under their arms and backpacks on their backs. The shops weren't open yet, but as we turned right at an intersection I heard and then noticed a Japanese woman in a flowing black kimono without an obi standing on the corner. Her long black hair was loose and was worn straight below her shoulders. She had a large strand of wooden beads in her hands, and there were some white papers lying at her feet. Her loud voice attracted one or two students. As they approached, she kneeled and pointed to the open papers, spoke even louder, and held one hand up in the air for emphasis. In the other hand, she held the beads.

I was fascinated and wanted to stay and watch her, but Mama-san discouraged me, moving away as quickly as she could. I can only surmise that this woman was a priestess, but I felt that Mama-san was protecting me, and I followed her lead.

The American Compound

The American compound, Mount Kurokuriyama, situated on top of the mountain, was surrounded by rolls of barbed wire on top of a cyclone fence, lush green plants, and rice paddies that were terraced down the mountainside. Sometimes we saw a farmer wearing a funnel-shaped straw hat walking his bicycle on the dirt road below our kitchen. The only thing separating us was the cyclone fence. As long as we lived there, we never saw him look up in our direction, and we never saw him smile. We never saw him riding his bicycle. He never responded to a loud hello or konichiwa (good afternoon) from groups of children in the neighborhood or from Frank and me. He did not acknowledge quiet stares or children waving to him, but we always knew it was 5:30 p.m. when we saw him walking his bicycle on the dirt road below the kitchen.

At the end of our street, there was an empty lot. Neighborhood children sometimes gathered there in the late afternoons to play ball, pull up bamboo shoots, and eat them as snacks—they tasted like celery hearts. When the sun began to set, the rays were so gorgeous, the colors so beautiful, we stood silently, staring at the curving beauty of the terraced mountains surrounding us, drinking in the beauty of Mount Kurokuriyama and the setting sun, and realizing how lucky we were.

In the compound, my mother was surrounded by other military wives who were home during the day. Sometimes I walked home for lunch and found a group of women sitting in the living room talking and my mother smiling. They played bridge together and sometimes they had lunch together, but not every day. My mother, like my father, was a reader and always had a book in her hand. The women belonged to the Officers' Wives organization and once a month had a luncheon at the Officer's Club. Sometimes my mother would ask me if she should wear a certain Sunday dress and shoes that matched her purse. Some of the ladies wore hats and gloves to the luncheons. Many of the women were young like my mother. Sometimes several of her friends would meet at our house and go to the luncheon together. This often involved conversations about their dress, hats, and whether their gloves matched their shoes. These were times that kept my mother from feeling lonely and homesick.

It was at one of those luncheons that she saw an Ikebana demonstration by a Japanese florist. She was so impressed by the demonstration that she bought some flower vases on the Japanese market and kept fresh flowers in the house regularly. My mother was very creative and arranging flowers gave her so much pleasure. I still have those unusual vases.

For me, living in the compound meant that I could take piano lessons from one of the officer's wives who had an upright piano in her living room. I practiced on the piano in the school auditorium, as did the few other piano students she had. My mother encouraged me to join the new Girl Scout troop in the compound. Periodically, we met with a Japanese Girl Scout troop in Nara. Once, both groups went on a joint bus ride to sketch nature pictures in a city park. The Japanese scouts wore light blue uniforms with maroon neck scarves and berets. We were a new scout troop, not organized long enough to have uniforms, and just wore our school clothes. People in the park were drawn to our joint gathering under a large tree and walked behind each scout making quiet comments about her work. The Japanese scouts were accomplished artists. Sadly, only two of our scouts exhibited any artistic talents. As each sketchbook was held up for a critique, the Japanese people who gathered to watch applauded enthusiastically for the best works and mumbled quietly when an undeveloped sketch was shown. When it was over, our bus driver took each Japanese scout to her home before driving us back to Mt. Kurokuriyama. One of the Japanese scouts sitting in the back of the small bus became ill from motion sickness and threw up. I was sorry for her, but glad for once that it wasn't me.

The newest residents in the compound were the most popular because they wore the most stylish clothes from the States and so did their children. They brought new recipes, magazines, books, and ideas for decorating. Their children had new games and toys that the rest of us wanted to try. They also brought news of politics and the events of the Korean War, which ended while we were living in Japan. Although there was a small movie theater in the compound, there was no radio or television, and everyone wanted to know from the new residents what was happening in the States.

Our life in Kurokuriyama was uneventful until a young girl across the street was struck with polio. There were five children in this central Texas family, and she was the youngest. With long, curly, blonde hair and large brown eyes, she was a beautiful child about six years old, always smiling and happy. Now a silent panic lived with every parent on our block. *If it happened to her, it could happen to any child.* My parents discussed sending us back to the States to live with my grandparents. Of course, my mother would go with us, but she didn't want to leave my father.

All children who had been in contact with her were ordered to take gamma-globulin shots. A friend of my mother's drove us to the front of the movie theater where the army bus was waiting for all the exposed children and their families. The bus would drive everyone to the large military hospital in Otsu for the inoculations. We boarded the bus and sat tensely with everyone else, wondering what the outcome of all this would be.

We had taken a battery of shots to get to Japan, and now we were ordered to take more. This fact wore on me during the hour-long journey to the hospital. By the time we reached Otsu, I was really frightened. Frank never said a word, but I knew he was equally frightened. It was not only the shot that frightened us, but the thought of getting polio as well. My cousin in Houston had contracted polio before we left for Japan. Now he sat in a wheelchair.

We had to wait in line when we arrived at the hospital, and this added to the agony of wondering what the shots would be like. I did not have to wonder very long. A stone-faced nurse, wearing a stiffly starched white hat and white uniform, jerked and pulled back a white curtain, exposing an empty gurney and a medic holding the longest needle I had ever seen. It was easily four or five inches long. That was too much for me, and I burst into tears. A chain reaction took place, and soon every child standing in line was crying. The father of a small boy in front of us looked up and frowned at me. My mother immediately chastised me. I stopped crying immediately, only to be called to take the first shots, one in each buttock. Frank was next, and then we left immediately for Nara.

The military parents who belonged to the Parent-Teacher Association (PTA) at our small school wanted their children to learn to speak and read Japanese to help us assimilate into Japanese culture. There were three grades in one room. A tutor was hired and came once a week to teach the upper grades to read and speak Japanese, but we actually had two tutors. The first one spoke "Oxford English," and with her Japanese accent, no one could understand her. She never smiled, but dressed formally in a kimono and an elaborate obi. Her demeanor was rigid and unfriendly. She did not appear to enjoy being with us. In a few weeks we had a second tutor who happened to be the same gentleman who gave Frank and me the puppy. He also dressed formally, in a black morning coat and English trousers, but he never stopped smiling. He engaged us and had us laughing and repeating the sounds that make up the Japanese language. Soon we were speaking Japanese and looking forward to weekly visits from this warm and friendly gentleman.

To further Japanese-American relationships, the American military wives wanted to involve the Japanese community in Nara with the American community on Mount Kurokuriyama. The American women invited a group of local Japanese women to visit their homes in the compound. My mother volunteered to have the eighty Japanese women come and tour our duplex as part of the cultural exchange.

A week before the women were to arrive, my mother and Hatsie were in a flurry of cleaning. Everything had to be just perfect. The windows had to be cleaned, the hardwood floors and silverware had to be polished until they shined, and everything in the house had to be dusted or washed. Frank and I had to take our shoes off at the door when we came in, and we could not sit on the sofa. We spent most of that week in our bedroom reading or playing games. In addition, my mother stayed in the kitchen all week, baking and reading recipes. Hatsie helped there too. I think they were both exhausted, but finally the special day arrived. My mother had an artistic talent for making the simplest things look special, and she loved to entertain. The dining-room table looked beautiful with fresh flowers, polished silverware, freshly pressed white linen napkins and white linen tablecloth, finger sandwiches, cut-up fruit, cookies, sweetbreads, nuts, and punch.

When I came home from school that day, there was an army bus parked in front of our duplex. My mother, wearing a beautiful dress, was standing at the door greeting the Japanese women, who were all wearing dark suits, white or beige blouses, stockings, dark high-heeled shoes, and carrying purses uncomfortably as they filed inside. I was told to go to my bedroom and stay there until the women left. Frank was already there reading a book on his bed. We were not to mess anything up, and we had to be quiet.

A line of Japanese women moved slowly from the front door into the dining room, snaking around the dining-room table, studying the food and punch, moving past the kitchen, back into the living room, down the hallway, into the bedrooms, and out the front door again. The women spoke in low voices among themselves, looking intently at everything in sight. As I moved to the hallway, I noticed one woman in the living room had large water stains on the lower pocket of her suit jacket. Water was dripping from her pocket onto the hardwood floor that Hatsie had polished to shine like a mirror. I spoke quietly to my mother about the water dripping on the floor. She said not to say anything to the lady but to go and get some paper towels and wipe up the water.

The woman looked down at the floor and then at her pocket as I quickly wiped up the dripping water. Her face turned beet red, and some of the women began to chastise her quietly. Other women frowned at her and the puddle on the floor. She smiled quickly at my mother, put her hand in her pocket, and took out several pieces of melting ice. I offered to take them from her and said a few words in Japanese. She seemed to recover from her embarrassing faux pas, but her face remained very red. The other women frowned and stood away from her as the line continued to move slowly through our duplex. Later, my mother mentioned that she must have taken the ice cubes in someone else's home because she had not been in our home long enough for the ice to melt.

When the last woman left, my mother sat down to relax. We talked about the woman who had pieces of ice in her pocket. My mother wondered if any of the other women took any items from the homes they'd visited and what the other women said to the "ice snatcher." The Japanese did not use ice for beverages. My mother concluded that the woman had never seen cubes of ice and did not know what they were. The women seemed to genuinely enjoy being in our house. Before leaving, each guest smiled warmly at my mother, which pleased her very much. We had homemade cookies, sweetbreads, and punch for a week because our Japanese visitors did not eat or drink any of the foods my mother prepared. In spite of this, she was delighted to have the Japanese women come into our home.

Americans on Mount Kurokuriyama made Christmas in Japan special. There were colored lights in the windows of the duplexes, and nearly everyone had a real Christmas tree decorated with colored lights and bright decorations. At school, we practiced singing Christmas carols and a Christmas pageant for the PTA program. I was asked to be an angel and stood with my arms extended while the choir sang, "Angels We Have Heard on High." All of this brought traditions from the States to our isolated community on top of the mountain. On Christmas morning, Frank and I found Japanese-made bicycles near the Christmas tree, and a small book, an English version, of traditional Japanese children's stories, Old Tales of Japan by Yuri Yasuda. We both loved this book. My father helped Frank learn to balance on his first two-wheeled bike. They were in the street in front of the duplex most of Christmas Day. My father pushed the bike and watched him balance, and then he ran to catch it before Frank fell or crashed. My cousin Helen taught me to ride her bike in Blytheville, Arkansas—I still have the scars on my knees to prove it—so I didn't have any trouble riding my shiny maroon bike. It even had handbrakes. I loved that bike, and I loved to ride so fast that my hair blew in the wind like it did when I stood next to my father on a ship's deck. When we transferred back to the States, we left our bikes in Japan. Hatsie might have taken them home to her brothers and sisters.

A Japanese School

Once we moved to Mt. Kurokuriyama, I could walk to school instead of riding the bus. Our principal, teachers, and the PTA believed we should be as familiar as possible with the Japanese culture. Throughout the year we took several field trips. Our principal, a pleasant woman who always smiled, arranged for us to visit a school within walking distance.

On the appointed day, we marched in single file with no particular behavioral reminders and proceeded down the dirt path on the mountainside until we reached the other school. As we approached the building, I listened for the sound of children laughing and bouncing balls, and tennis shoes pounding loose dirt; there was no sound at all. It was strangely quiet. We were greeted warmly at the door by an official dressed in a black, Western-style suit, who showed us into the freezing building and into a small conference room. There he spoke quietly and briefly, advising us that the students were all in class and to please proceed quietly to the fifth-grade classroom.

We entered the classroom, whose floor-to-ceiling windows were open all the way. There were no spaces between the wooden desks. There was hardly enough space to stand in the back of the room. Thirty or more students were sitting with straight backs and hands folded on their desks, eyes glued to the front of the room and feet flat on the floor. There was a clean slate chalkboard behind the teacher, a young Japanese man dressed in a black, Western-style sport coat with a long-sleeved shirt open at the collar. His feet, propped up on the desk (which was clear of papers, pens, pencils, or any decorative items), were protected by Western-style, shiny, black-laced shoes. His hands were folded in his lap, and his eyes were closed.

A young student stood in front of the desk giving the lesson; he read from a book and periodically looked up at the other students. Except for the wind whipping through the open windows, not a sound could be heard in the classroom or in the building. No one moved. The children did not appear to be breathing, just listening intently to the presentation. We stood freezing in awe and disbelief as cold wind blew through the open windows.

Soon, the teacher opened his eyes and removed his feet from the desk. Before he moved his chair, the students immediately stood up simultaneously and began to march out of the room in single file. Not a word was spoken.

All the students were bundled in thick coats and pants, but they wore getas on their bare feet. Several Japanese students had inchworms of green snot under their noses. I took a tissue from my coat pocket and wiped the nose of one student who was in front of me, even though he had a shocked look on his face. The Japanese teacher frowned and looked down at his desk. I moved aside and the line of students passed out of the room. Looking back, I wonder what the repercussions of my impulsive behavior were for that student.

Afterward, we were invited into the conference room and served hot tea. Our principal spoke with the official of the school. We expressed our thanks for the tea and the warm welcome to the school. Then we departed for the dirt path and the top of Mount Kurokuriyama.

When we returned to our classroom, we spent the afternoon writing thank-you notes to the Japanese schoolchildren. We talked among ourselves all afternoon about the cold, the silence, and the obedience we observed. Our teacher wanted to know if we could learn better if we left the windows open during the winter months. "No!" everyone replied. She also asked us if we could remain that quiet all day. We said no, we could not, but we would try to be quieter.

On another field trip, still in winter, we visited an ice factory in downtown Nara. It was cold enough for us to wear our winter coats, but the inside of the ice factory was like a deep freeze. The men who worked there wore layers of thick, heavy coats and hats that covered the head and neck. Thick gloves covered their hands. No one smiled; no one spoke. We were led from one fascinating machine to another. Smoke from dry ice puffed out of huge vats. I had the distinct feeling that the workers were annoyed with us standing around watching them. I spoke a few words in Japanese to one of the men standing over a large vat. His eyes never left the vat. His posture never wavered, but he uttered a curt, "Hai" (Yes).

On our last field trip we went to an observatory, but now my memory has faded, and I cannot recall the name of the observatory or the city. It was early spring, and we were all wearing coats or jackets. We rode the train for an hour and a half up into the mountains. It stopped at nearly every small town where Japanese people of all ages boarded and disembarked. Our car was crowded and we stood, giving older people a chance to sit down. The passengers kept looking at us and talking among themselves. It was unusual to see Caucasian children in Japan at that time. We arrived mid-morning and walked to the observatory from the train station.

The telescope was in a large, domed-shaped room. There were a few small pictures of planets and stars hanging randomly on the walls. The room was dark, and the telescope was so large I was afraid to look into it. I didn't know what to do and walked outside to look at the mountaintops where the sun was shining and the wind was blowing. No one else seemed to be interested in the outside so I went back inside. I was ready to leave, but no one else was. The Japanese astronomers seemed delighted to have us at the observatory. During our visit they smiled and chatted constantly among themselves. One of them spoke English, and our principal seemed to be his friend.

We brought our lunches with us and sat outside on the concrete walkway to eat. With snow-covered mountains in the background, we had a beautiful "lunchroom." After eating lunch, I was bored and ready to leave again. Science was not my favorite subject. I needed more explanation about what I was expected to see in the observatory and the telescope. The trip back to Nara was equally uneventful, but we talked constantly while the moving train kept us swinging from one side of the car to the other, giving the Japanese passengers stories to tell about the American schoolchildren who also rode the train that day.

During the cold weather months, we played in the gym, but as spring-like weather became hot and humid toward the end of the school year, we were allowed to go outside and play after lunch. There was no cafeteria, and everyone brought a lunch from home. We also went outside for recess in the afternoon. We ran, played chase, played on the see-saws, and climbed on the jungle gym. Sometimes we played softball during recess, but after all that running around in the heat everyone was hot, sweaty, and thirsty when we came inside. There was always a race to see who could get to the water fountain first, boys or girls. Everyone else waited patiently in line for a much-needed drink of cool water.

It took a while to get a drink, because three-inch roaches—so common in Nara—accumulated in the dampness of the basin in the water fountain; they were also hoping for a cool bit of water. Each person had to wave his or her hand to scatter them away from the fountain before turning on the water. The roaches spread their large wings and flew around the group of sweaty students, landing on the ones closest to the source of water. No one screamed or jumped when they landed on our clothing, arms, or hair. We just kept swatting to keep them moving. The only problem was that once they landed, they stuck, because their legs and feet had sticky hairs on them that kept the roaches attached to anything they touched.

A Sunday Drive

We dressed in our Sunday-best clothes to go for a ride. After all, it was Sunday, even though we did not attend church services. My mother always looked beautiful and dressed well. She wore black patent-leather pumps with her flowered dress. Frank wore dress pants, a white shirt with a bow tie, and a jacket. I wore my pink Easter dress and white lace socks with patent-leather shoes. My father wore a jacket, white shirt with a bow tie, and dress pants. His shoes were as shiny as a new penny. We left the base and headed down the mountain into Nara, then out into the countryside. Usually we had an idea of where we were going but not always. Today was no different. My father wasn't a talker. He just told my mother we were going for a ride.

I do not remember how we were permitted to enter the premises. I only remember that my father drove into the area and turned off the car engine. None of us said anything. The deadened earth was the blackest black I had ever seen. Devastation stretched from one side of the horizon to the other. *Why is he taking us here*, I wondered. I hoped we wouldn't go any farther. I wanted to go home. Twisted, misshapen pieces of melted metal and rock were strewn randomly across the surface. We sat in stunned silence and stared in disbelief at the scorched, lifeless, blackened environment that stretched as far as the eye could see. My mother sat motionless, staring out of the windshield. Frank was frozen to his seat, staring out of the side window. *What is this place? It's like we're not even on Earth.*

Out of nowhere a group of shouting, shabbily dressed Japanese men appeared, storming our car. *What had we done?* I was seized with terror. Some of the men were carrying signs printed in red Japanese letters. The car was surrounded by angry faces and moving bodies blocking our view of the horror surrounding us, which terrified my mother. Calling my father's name, she said she wanted to leave immediately. Rocks started bouncing off the car windows and doors. Frank and I, paralyzed with fear, were speechless, motionless. The men in front began to rock our car. My mother started to cry, begging my father to leave. Her tears frightened me as much as the men outside. I wondered what would happen to us if the men opened our doors and dragged us out. I had never seen anger like this. We were trapped. *Would they beat us, hit us with the placards?* Outside angry voices kept rising; inside, my mother's voice kept rising, begging my father to leave.

Rocking back and forth, higher and higher, I thought our car was going to turn over. I have never experienced so much terror. My father sat, like a piece of stone, fearless, and emotionless, looking out of the left window. I kept waiting for him to calm my mother, to disperse the men somehow, and drive us away, but he just sat, stone-faced, and stared out of the left window. The men were throwing the car down so hard. *Was it was it going to break into pieces?* When the front end went down, the back springs flew up, and the car seemed to be flying until our heads hit the ceiling. Then the pattern was reversed, and my parents hit their heads on the ceiling. *Was the car going to turn over from front to back or back to front?* I sat behind my father, terrified, staring in disbelief as he ignored my mother's pleas. He never even blinked. His green eyes turned to cold, gray steel and bore into the eyes of the Japanese men. *How could he let this happen to us? Why did he bring us here? Why was he ignoring my mother's pleas? Was he thinking of the bombs that hit the British train he was riding in northern England during the war? Was he thinking of the bomb that exploded in front of him as he was leaving a chemist's shop in London?*

The men exposed their teeth and became ferocious wild animals, shrieking, shouting, banging the car windows, rocking us from side to side, lifting the car up high, letting it drop hard. Loose objects became missiles that were hurled at us. Never have I experienced such anger. Never had I seen my mother so upset or my father so aloof and reserved. How I wished I could help my mother, but my body would not move. I wondered if we would get out there alive.

I whispered to Frank, "Quick, get down on the floor and cover your head." As we dropped to the floor, I saw my mother's hands shaking my father's arm. I kept saying my prayers and keeping an eye on the angry assailants. Outside, I saw one man, standing by my mother's window observing our actions inside the car. He kept frowning at my mother, wringing his hands. He did not join the group's actions against us, but I was still alarmed.

The men acknowledged my father's defiance or indifference. He could not, would not be provoked and their actions began to subside. The missiles fell from their hands. Voices subdued, and the car sat still. The man closely watching my mother looked as if he might weep. He smiled sadly, briefly to me, still on the floor, turned his back, and walked away, the last man to leave our car. *Would they come back and attack us again? Were they waiting for us to leave so they could attack us from the behind? Were they trying to disable our car and make us more vulnerable?*

My mother sat still in the quiet and kept blowing her nose, wiping her eyes, catching her breath. Inching up slowly to see if it was safe, I put my hand on Frank's shoulder. Cautiously, we slid back into our seats. The men were nowhere in sight. Quiet returned to the inside of the car. My father turned his head and stared out of the front windshield. He sat still for a moment, studied the horizon from left to right, started the car, and let it idle. Then we began to move forward, slowly, moving away from the blackened, deadened landscape and the men who attacked our car, and headed back toward Nara. No one talked; no one moved. I kept looking at my mother and Frank. I was shocked that my father ignored her, that he didn't seem concerned about Frank or me. Why did he take us to Hiroshima?

I realize the tragic significance of the Atomic Bomb . . . It is an awful responsibility which has come to us . . . We thank God that it has come to us, instead of our enemies; and we pray that He may guide us to use it in His ways and for His purposes.
—President Harry S. Truman, August 9, 1945

As we drove through the countryside covered with green rice paddies, the late afternoon sun fell to the horizon. As we reached the city, we could see the gold sphere on top of the five-story pagoda. We passed Nara Park, where families stood feeding the deer and the old mama-sans fed koi in the large pond. We headed up the side of the mountain to the American compound. As we passed through the barbed-wire and cyclone-fence security gates of Mount Kurokuriyama, my father showed his military ID. The Japanese guard, wearing khakis, a white helmet, a white scarf tucked in his neck, and white gloves saluted my father before we passed through the gate. In the backseat, I watched the sunset through the mountains and longed to return to our life in the old two-storied house in downtown Nara. I wanted to have tea with Mama-san and hear her quiet, gentle voice singing my name.

Ah So Deska? (Is That So?)

On a Sunday afternoon my father called me away from reading *Heidi* in the bedroom I shared with Frank, and sent me to the small PX to buy a quart of strawberry ice cream, my favorite kind. I was so happy to be outside and ride my bike to the other side of the compound for any reason. Wind rustled the pine needles and blew through my hair as I pumped hard and fast to get up and down rolling streets. Bird calls echoed through the trees. This was a happy day for me. I felt as free as a bird flying through the pine trees. I parked my bike in the rack in front of the PX and walked through the door, panting like a dog because I had pumped my bike so hard. Jake, the Japanese cashier, handed over a pint of strawberry ice cream in a brown paper bag. I put the change and the receipt in the bag to keep from losing it on the way home, and then came the hard part—pumping uphill.

On the way back, I had to pump most of the way uphill with one hand on the handlebars while the other hand clutched the brown paper bag with the ice cream. I huffed and I puffed while I pumped, standing on the pedals. The bike veered left, then right, barely moving, and then almost rolled backward before I could straighten it out and move forward a little at a time. When I turned onto our street, I was breathless. Sweat from the ice-cream carton soaked my jacket and shirt and dripped down onto my jeans. I could almost taste the ice cream, soft now and runny the way I really like it. I couldn't wait to get to the front door. Just a few more blocks.

A dark-green military police jeep whizzed by just as I approached the curve in the street where our duplex was situated. I glanced inside the jeep as it passed by and was surprised to see a medium-sized, light-colored dog in the back seat. A long red tongue hung out of its mouth. Large brown eyes stared blankly from behind the helmeted MP (military policeman) in the front seat. That wasn't my Eppy. He was at home tied up to the persimmon tree. Why would MPs be driving around with a dog on the back seat of a jeep anyway? Perhaps it was some new procedure; things were always changing at the base.

I pulled up to the curb and looked for Eppy, my best friend, who greeted me affectionately whenever I appeared. His chain hung from the persimmon tree. I walked over to the tree in the hope that Eppy had just gotten loose, but there was no evidence of that. Someone had clearly removed the chain from his collar. Now I realized it was Eppy in the back of the jeep.

Shaking, I walked in the door, headed for the kitchen, dropped the soft gooey ice-cream carton in the wet and torn paper bag on the counter, and went straight to my room.

"Don't you want some ice cream?" my father asked innocently.

"Somebody took Eppy! I don't want any ice cream!" I yelled. After some parents complained that Eppy was biting their children, my father had no choice but to give Eppy away, although nothing had been mentioned to me. Frank was home when the MPs came to take the dog. He was devastated by this loss.

I walked to the bedroom and lay down on my bed convulsing in dry tears. My best friend who loved me as much as I loved him was gone. I was all alone now.

Sue Ellen was the new girl who sat in front of me at school. I went out of my way to make her feel welcome. She was from Florida, and I was from Houston. We shared stories of our home life during recess and lunchtime. Sometimes I rode my bicycle to her duplex on Saturdays because she didn't have a bicycle. Sue Ellen lived with her mother, stepfather, and stepbrother.

Our common thread was that we were always in trouble with our fathers. We never did anything right. My father was especially hard on me during evening meals. He accused me of playing with my food, taking bites that were too large, being too slow to finish eating, using my silverware incorrectly, putting my milk glass in the wrong place, or not passing a vegetable dish with two hands. He bellowed a constant barrage of criticism toward me at every evening meal. I dreaded five o'clock every evening while I was setting the table. My mother's eyes never left my father's face when he was so critical. Maybe she was afraid to stand up to him, or maybe she didn't know how. Maybe she didn't want to confront him in front of us. He was a large man with a powerful physique. Maybe she was afraid of him. Whatever the reason, I felt so alone, afraid, and the criticisms stung even more. There were other times when he was not happy with me, but I didn't know why. I wondered if he didn't know what to do with me. When I was out of my room, he yelled at me and wanted to know what I was doing. I worked hard to stay out of his sight.

When I look back now, I wonder if the responsibility of his work was taking a toll on him. He was a company commander, but at the time, I did not know this. He often talked to my mother outside on the kitchen steps. If they were inside, we were sent to our bedroom. Sometimes my parents sat in the living room, and my father talked while my mother listened. We were not to interrupt them when he did, but I watched from another room as they sat together. He spoke angrily and animatedly. My mother listened attentively and then spoke quietly while my father listened passively. He seemed to really need her when they talked like this after supper.

In Sue Ellen's case, her stepfather heavily favored his son. She was left to do dishes and housework. She felt that no one cared about her. After discussing our dilemma for weeks, we finally decided to solve our problems by running away from home.

The following Saturday I told my mother I was riding to Sue Ellen's house and biked to her duplex with a fresh batch of mayonnaise-and-saltine-cracker sandwiches, some Snicker bars I'd bought at the small PX with my allowance, and my stash of Bazooka bubblegum. I parked my bicycle in front of her house and knocked on the door. She was ready to go. She told her mother we were going for a walk. She didn't have any snacks with her because her mother was always in the kitchen. Dressed alike in jeans, a T-shirt, tennis shoes and socks, we headed for the woods.

As soon as the housing area was out of sight, we crossed the street and took the first path we found heading into the woods, a place we had never explored. The wind was blowing just enough to disturb the tall, majestic pines. It wasn't long before we felt cold. As we climbed up the mountain, we saw interesting rocks, leaves, unusual plants, and large bugs with lots of legs. Sue Ellen remained quiet, but gradually I began to feel very unsettled. Neither of us knew where we were going or what we would do when we arrived there. After sometime we reached the top of the mountain. Hidden by trees and large rocks, we looked down at what appeared to be an American army post surrounded by a tall, barbed-wire fence. We saw a fleet of green army jeeps and trucks parked in front of a good-sized, yellow-brick building. A large number of men dressed in camouflage uniforms were standing in formation. Sitting in fine red dirt, we ate the saltine-cracker-and-mayonnaise sandwiches in silence while we watched the activity below. Was this where our fathers went to work every day? My father was picked up in a jeep every morning and driven to the post in downtown Nara. He wore a dress uniform every day.

We watched as the formations broke without warning as men began to move quickly to the trucks and jeeps. Engines idled. Jeeps began driving off the post as groups of soldiers ran and jumped into the back of moving trucks. Some of the trucks were rolling out of the cyclone gate of the post. Suddenly, a large, dome-shaped yellow bug, covered with large black spots, lots of legs, and open wings, jumped on my arm and stuck there. I screamed at the top of my lungs. The reality of all this became too much for me. I felt that there was an emergency, and the men were being called to take care of it. I could see my parents leaving Nara or even Japan without me. I would be left in the woods to survive alone with Sue Ellen and the large yellow bug. "STOP!" I screamed. "DON'T GO! PLEASE, DON'T GO! TAKE ME WITH YOU! DON'T LEAVE ME!" I sobbed. The truck engines were making so much noise I couldn't even hear Sue Ellen. What would happen if the soldiers did hear me screaming? Would we be arrested and taken to jail? Surely we would be in deep trouble at home.

I wanted Mama-san and my grandparents. Sue Ellen tried to console me, but the thought of living in the woods forever was unthinkable. I was ready to go back to whatever it was I was running away from. At least there were no bugs at home, and I didn't have to eat mayonnaise-and-saltine-cracker sandwiches every day. Besides, it was uncharacteristic of me to run from my problems. Slowly, I began to regain my composure. The tears dried. Sue Ellen helped pack up the rest of the cracker sandwiches. I was cold and afraid. I couldn't wait to get out of the woods. We started backtracking our way to the dirt path. I stumbled down the path to the sidewalk. Sue Ellen followed slowly behind me. I asked her to look closely at my face. By the time we were in the sunlight, the redness in my face had disappeared. No one could tell that I had been crying. We weren't going to live in the woods, and we had no place to go but home. Sue Ellen was not anxious to return to her home and neither was I, but we would have a bug-free bed to sleep in and were guaranteed three meals a day.

When I returned home, I acted as if nothing had happened. I was not questioned about my visit to Sue Ellen's. Nothing had changed at home, but I decided to try not to be so sensitive to my father's criticism. My parents never knew of our failed adventure. The issue of discipline was critical for military families. Anyone who could not control his children would be sent back to the States, dishonorably. Military children were well aware of this issue.

About two weeks later as I lay in bed, I heard the sound of bicycle bells moving up and down the street in front of our duplex. The phone rang about 9:00 p.m. that night. My mother came into the bedroom and asked me if I knew anything about Sue Ellen. Her mother called to say she had not come home after school and the MPs were out looking for her. *So she finally did run away*, I thought. I hoped she was safe. I was too afraid of the dark to run away at night. I said a prayer for Sue Ellen and hoped she would be safe wherever she was. The next day she was not at school. Eventually, Sue Ellen did return. Nobody would have anything to do with her when she came back. That same week her mother came to school after class was dismissed, told the students that Sue Ellen had been punished enough, and asked everyone to be more considerate of her.

But Sue Ellen was still ostracized. It was as if she were not even in the classroom. No one spoke to her, looked at her, or asked her to stand next to them in line. My heart ached for her, and I was lonely without her to talk to. I was ashamed of myself, but my mother told me not to have anything to do with her. Maybe she was afraid I would be influenced by Sue Ellen's behavior.

My father became less and less approachable when we lived in the duplex on Mount Kurokuriyama. Sometimes after supper, my parents would sit on the concrete stoop outside the kitchen. My mother would listen closely as my father talked. I can only assume that these conversations concerned his role and work as company commander. Frank and I were not allowed to interrupt them or come into the room during these times. He was always angry and sharp in his remarks to me. I felt that I never did anything right. Frank, on the other hand, usually could do no wrong, but not always.

One Saturday about noon, a friend and I walked from her duplex to mine. We were going to have mayonnaise-and-saltine-cracker sandwiches for lunch in my front yard. It was hot and humid outside. Everybody had their windows open to let air in. We both wore shorts and sandals. Gnats zipped around our faces and landed on our shoulders. As we came close to the yard we heard the sound of someone tenderizing meat, loudly. Then I heard a yelp and I knew it wasn't meat. I told my friend I had to go home and see about my little brother. "What did he do?" she asked. I said I didn't know, but I had to go

There was no sound inside as I approached the front screen door quietly and removed my shoes so no one would hear me entering the house. I looked around to see if either of my parents were in the living room or kitchen. The coast was clear. Carrying my sandals I tiptoed to the hallway; again, the coast was clear. I tiptoed slowly and quietly to our bedroom and looked in. There was Frank wadded up in a ball in the middle of his bed, sucking his thumb hard. He was as white as a sheet. I walked quietly over to him, bent over and whispered, asking him if he wanted a drink of water. He stopped sucking his thumb, said yes, and started sucking hard again. I retraced my steps to the kitchen very quietly and brought him a glass of water, which he gulped down. I asked him if he wanted another drink, and again he said yes. I retraced my steps again and returned with the water. I asked him if he was going to be all right. When he said yes, I lay down on my bed and started reading a book.

I never knew what happened between my father and Frank, who was only six years old. Not long afterward, my mother was very sick. My father called a military doctor who lived close by one evening to come over and see her because she couldn't get out of bed. She seemed sad and melancholy for a long time, but nothing was ever said about this incident with Frank, which only made me more afraid of my father. I avoided him whenever possible, which was difficult in our small duplex, but I did not want to feel that belt on my legs.

Hatsie was my best friend and confidante during our tenure in Nara. Every day when I came home from school she was there to greet me and listen to me talk about my day. Even though we both knew she did not understand most of what I was saying, she listened willingly and sympathetically.

She was curious about American customs and the geography of the United States. Sometimes when we were the only ones at home, she asked me why Americans did things in a certain way. Once she pulled a newspaper picture of a small Midwestern American city out of her pocket. With great excitement she pointed to the lights in the tall buildings and asked, "Mary-san"—she referred to me as Mary-san—"this New York? Look like this?"

"Yes," I replied, "it looks like that."

Hatsie learned to speak English fluently while she worked for us. She sometimes asked questions about the food we ate and about the way we sat at the table. When my father had to stay overnight at the base, which was rare, Hatsie stayed and prepared supper for my mother. It was usually an omelet with fresh vegetables, and it was always delicious. My mother depended on Hatsie a great deal and loved her as a daughter.

Sayonara

My mother accompanied me to school for the Christmas program in mid-December, and afterward I said a tearful good-bye to all my teachers, who wished me well. After a flurry of packing, sorting things out, giving things to Hatsie, and leaving other things to be thrown away, our duplex became an empty reminder of a life we once lived. The Japanese movers carefully packed breakable items into large heavy-cardboard cylinders stuffed with straw. Each end was secured by a sturdy piece of metal. The cylinders were stenciled with my father's name, rank, and serial number. A new Stateside APO address was stenciled underneath. As our home life was being disassembled, we faced the uncertainty of what our new life would be like.

During our last summer in Nara, some cities in central Japan experienced unexpected flooding due to high typhoon activity. Using heavy equipment and soldiers from the base to relieve the flooding and build roads, my father helped many Japanese people who were left homeless. The mayors of these cities presented certificates to my father, expressing gratitude and thanks for his help. With great care, my father packed ten framed certificates, beautifully written in Japanese, to hang in his next office. The Japanese men who worked for my father at the base presented him with an old silk painting of a samurai warrior as a farewell gift. It seemed so appropriate for a soldier who was a warrior at heart. My father was very moved by these touching gifts.

Movers completed packing our belongings in one day, and our duplex was nearly empty, a shell of our former lives. In the morning, a driver arrived in an army sedan and stowed our luggage in the trunk while neighbors appeared outside for one last good-bye. Like little soldiers, we got into the back seat of the car without talking. My father sat in the front and waved to our neighbors through the window. My mother sat between us in the back and waved as the car pulled away heading to the train station where our luggage was checked and placed aboard the train.

My father's commanding officer and some of the officers who worked directly with my father came to see us off. "Good-bye" meant we would never see these particular people again. It was hard for my mother to say good-bye so many times. Sometimes I felt we spent our whole life just saying good-bye to people so we could meet more people. In fact, our life did seem to work that way. I knew better than to show any emotion in front of my father. Any sign of emotion made him very angry. A good soldier never showed emotion because this was considered a sign of weakness. An enemy could easily crack and wear down a man who showed emotion, easily aiding the enemy. Perhaps he felt he was protecting us by thinking of us as soldiers.

I held my tears in and reflected on the wonder of living in the old Japanese house, drinking green tea and shopping with Mama-san, visiting the Japanese school, riding the bullet train to Kyoto with Hatsie and Harumi, meeting Hatsie's family, feeding the deer and koi in Nara Park. I would miss seeing terraced rice fields and beautiful sunsets in Kurokuriyama and speaking Japanese.

With farewells and good wishes behind us, we boarded the train to Yokohama. Frank and I stored our treasured books, new crayons, and snacks in our compartment, sitting opposite each other next to the window. No one spoke as my father closed the door to the compartment, sat down, and took a long deep breath. The heavy emotions of moving and saying good-bye once again clung to all of us. The whistle blew. The train jerked slightly, was still for a moment, and then very slowly started moving out of the station while we sat in disbelief that our life was over once again.

Suddenly, there were shouts outside our window. The train was barely moving, but there was little Hatsie, in a Western-style dress coat, her face red and swollen from crying, tears streaming down her porcelain skin, her mouth forming all of our names, sobbing desperately, "Don't go! Don't go!" My parents jumped up. We all crowded around the window, wishing we could stop the train and get off, but it was moving too fast. Silent tears rolled down my mother's cheeks. Frank and I watched helplessly in horror. My stomach clenched. What would happen to Hatsie? The train was moving faster, but Hatsie kept running after us, calling our names, her face stretched with pain, hands grasping in the air as if she were trying to catch time and hold it still. "Jesus, I hope she doesn't fall," my father said quietly. Then she appeared as a spot moving on the concrete, the next minute she was gone forever as the train kept moving so fast it felt as if we weren't moving at all. We sat down slowly. The compartment remained quiet for a long, long time.

We got off the train in Yokohama and checked into a small hotel the military used to board incoming and outgoing personnel and their families. The next morning we woke early and sat down for a good breakfast that would hold us until the dining salon on the ship opened for lunch. My parents and I had eggs, bacon, toast, and juice. My parents also had several cups of coffee. Frank had his usual cheeseburger with french fries and a Coke. It gave him so much pleasure when he had these foods for breakfast. I was feeling alone, anxious about getting on the ship, very sad about leaving Japan, and anxious about crossing the Pacific again because I was motion sick whenever we traveled. We finished with breakfast and headed slowly toward the ship. I followed my parents up the gangplank and into the lobby, breathed in the strong odor of diesel fuel, and threw up.

My parents, one on either side of me, were very embarrassed. They turned and looked in the opposite direction. Frank looked like he didn't know who we were. I was so humiliated that I wanted to hide. We didn't even have our room assignment yet. Military and civilian persons carrying suitcases were moving all around us, and there I stood with a large, irregular-shaped puddle of vomit between my feet. Some of it had splashed onto my socks and shoes. Some of it had splashed onto the bottom of my dress. I needed a tissue to wipe my face. My parents were not happy, but it turned out to be a good thing for them because we were taken to our room before anyone else. Frank and I were each assigned a top bunk, but I was told to lie down on a lower bunk and remove my shoes and socks. I was so grateful to be in the bunk bed. I traveled across the Pacific Ocean lying in that lower bunk during the day, periodically sipping hot, flat Coke, and nibbling on stale saltine crackers.

The sea was so turbulent during our December crossing from Yokohama to San Francisco and so very cold that it was impossible to walk on the deck after we were at sea. My parents insisted that I get up, dress, and go to the salon for dinner every evening. Afterward, I walked back to the room and usually threw up everything I had eaten, including all the flat Coke and stale saltines I had consumed that day. Fortunately, I was the only one in the family who experienced motion sickness. Periodically, the ocean calmed enough for us to walk out on deck after supper, dressed in warm coats and scarves, before heading back to our cabin. One moonless night we stood together in total darkness at the ship's rail, searching for the horizon, the sea, or the sky, but we could only hear the sea slapping the side of the ship. It was disorienting and frightening, and it was the blackest black I have ever seen.

We had lifeboat drills on deck at the same time every day. Attendance was required for every passenger. Roll was taken by a crewman. No one was allowed to talk. Each passenger was assigned to a certain spot on one of the decks. Families were assigned together. In the event of fire or an "abandon ship" order, passengers would know where to go to board a lifeboat. Sometimes during the drills, lifeboats would be lowered into the Pacific and then pulled back up and secured in place above the deck. During one drill, a crewman took a lifeboat out from the ship, making a large circle some distance away from the ship before coming back again. Like a child's plastic toy, the lifeboat tossed around between windblown waves. We stood and watched in an anxious silence as the young man in a light-blue shirt and dark-blue pants grew smaller and smaller. Would the rough water allow him to return to the ship? With some skilled maneuvering, he returned safely. Being tossed around in a lifeboat was one thing that every passenger dreaded.

Sometimes in the morning I went out on deck for fresh air after breakfast. Once I saw my father standing all alone next to the railing, his hands in his pockets, staring at the horizon. Usually he would be smoking a cigarette, but I watched him for a moment as he stood motionless and appeared deep in thought. He seemed to be in another place. I walked over and stood next to him. The cold wind whipped through my hair. White caps slapped the side of the ship one after another. We rocked from side to side as the MSTS ship moved steadily through the churning Pacific waters. I stood closer to my father. I don't think he knew I was next to him, but when I reached up and put my arm in the crook of his elbow, the corner of his lips curled upward briefly. He never took his eyes off the water. Together we stood silently until he abruptly turned and said, "Let's go inside." He wasn't wearing a coat and must have been cold.

This encouraged me to go out on deck again the next afternoon. This time I noticed a Japanese family standing on deck. They were watching the water, talking quietly among themselves. I kept my distance and when they moved away from the railing, I bowed my head and said good morning to them in Japanese, "Ohio Gozimashita." They were very surprised to hear me speaking Japanese and responded the same way. We had a warm conversation about where we lived and where we were going and then parted in the Japanese manner. The next time I saw them on the deck, my parents and Frank were standing on deck with me. We greeted each other in Japanese, then the gentleman handed me a small geisha doll in a glass case and wished that good luck would follow me throughout my life. I was so flattered, and my parents were very moved at this kind gesture. They spoke with my parents briefly before moving on. At times the Pacific was so violent that the ship was tossed up and down like a child's toy. The crew tied ropes along the railings inside the lobby and the hallways. Sometimes we walked at a forty-five-degree angle. We crossed the international dateline once again and celebrated Christmas twice. The ship's crew put up a small, artificial silver tree in the dining salon. There was a stocking filled with candy for each child on board. We were glad to be heading stateside, but it hardly seemed like Christmas, being seasick and not being with our family or close friends. We still missed our Hatsie and wondered what her life might be like now. Did she go to work for another American family? Was she at home helping her mother prepare food for the coming New Year? Sadly, we would never know, but we carried wonderful memories of Hatsie's kindness in our hearts.

It took us ten days to get to the port of San Francisco. My father's oldest brother and his family came to meet us. They drove us to their home in Tracy, a suburb of San Francisco. We stayed for nearly ten days while my parents waited for the new Ford they had ordered before leaving Nara. One evening, my aunt's parents invited us to their home. It was the closest we had been to a family group since we had left Houston in 1952, when we had lived with my grandparents. I can't remember how many people came to see us that evening, but it was great fun, and everyone wanted to know what it was like living in Japan.

When we left San Francisco we headed southeast, driving through the Mojave Desert, and then south through Arizona so we could see the Painted Desert and the Petrified Forest. My parents were proud of the new Ford. We had to be extra careful not to make any marks on the seats or the floor mats. As we arrived at the California border, we were stopped by the border police. Our car was inspected for fresh fruits and vegetables, and we were reminded not to transport agricultural products across the border. My parents answered questions about where we had been and what our destination was before we were allowed to drive away, but as soon as my father showed his military identification, the questions stopped and we were waved on. This action was repeated as we crossed each border between New Mexico, Arizona, and Texas. As we drove through the Southwest, Frank and I passed the time by studying the gorgeous cloud formations and trying to identify familiar shapes and forms in the clouds. We stared in disbelief at the red formations and wide, open spaces of the desert near the Petrified Forest. I could not begin to imagine how many small tile-roofed Japanese houses could fit into that beautiful space. Hatsie would be astonished at the sight of the red dirt, the mountainous shapes, the constant wind, and the vast, empty spaces. At the Petrified Forest my father pulled off the highway to give us a closer look at the glistening rock logs while the setting sun painted the desert in beautiful shades of orange, pink, yellow, and lavender. The sun kept sinking and kept changing colors as we stood silently absorbing the beauty of the desert. Somehow it seemed like a magnificent welcome-home gift from nature.

We drove from New Mexico and Arizona west into El Paso, Texas, and from there we drove for three days to reach Houston. I was carsick the entire trip. My father was unhappy that I was sick in the new car. From sun up to sun down, my father stayed on course, stopping only to go to the bathroom, when it was time to eat, or to get gas. As we approached downtown Houston, my mother wept quietly. She had been very homesick. Frank and I looked out of the windows in disbelief at the neon lights, new skyscrapers, and all the cars whizzing by us on the Houston highways. About one o'clock in the morning, we drove down Newcastle Avenue to Jonathan Street. Just before we turned onto Jonathan Street, a lonely car slowly passed us. The people inside waved at us warmly, but drove on. Then we realized my great-aunt, uncle, and cousin were driving home from my grandparents' house after waiting for some time to see us. We met with them several days later.

My father parked in front of the house and turned the engine off. We sat still in the quiet darkness, listening to the sound of crickets hiding in the grass. It was hard to believe that we were finally home. We looked at the porch light and the azaleas in the flower beds, the bird bath in the middle of the front yard, my grandfather's car parked in the driveway. In the darkness, the house and the yard looked the same as they did when we last saw them, making it even harder to believe that we had ever left. We walked quietly to the front door of my grandparents' house, which opened before we could even knock. My grandfather stood alone, just looking at us, and when my mother embraced her father, he wept hard. "It's so good to be home," my mother said through her tears. My grandfather kept wiping his eyes, but shook hands with my father. My mother, the eldest daughter, had come home again. My grandmother, wiping her eyes as my mother embraced her, lit up like a small Christmas tree. She kept hugging us, remarking how much we had grown, how thin we looked. We had been traveling for a month and eating irregularly. In the next few days, we saw our whole family—my mother's brothers and sisters and their children, in addition to a multitude of cousins. There were family dinners and catch-up time with our cousins. While we were there, my father took a few days to drive to Fort Hood, report for duty, and look for a house to rent in central Texas near the fort. Sixty miles from Fort Hood he found a house in Lampasas. He would carpool to the fort with other military men who lived in Lampasas.

While my father was away, I spent time with my cousins, Anna, thirteen, and Susan, twelve, who were closest to my age. I was eleven. They had boyfriends but could only go to church with them on Sunday evenings. They wore full skirts with lots of petticoats that showed when they walked. Their skirts made jingling sounds every time they moved because they pinned small silver bells underneath the petticoats. They wore peasant-style blouses with the full skirts and loafers with bobby socks. They wore necklaces, earrings, bracelets, and an ankle bracelet around one ankle. Red fingernail polish accented their fingers and toes. They knew how to do the bop, and they could sing all the words to Elvis Presley's songs. One had a portable radio, and the other had a record player. They both collected records, and both listened to the radio stations before going to sleep at night.

I felt so out of place in the jumper my mother had made for me and the lace-up saddle oxfords with thick white socks. I couldn't think of anything but Mama-san and Hatsie. I wanted to speak Japanese to them and offer them a persimmon, but of course that wasn't possible and would only make me appear very peculiar. When they sang Elvis Presley's songs to me, I sang Japanese songs to myself and thought how sad it was that they did not know anything about Japan or any Japanese. How could they? I was the one who had lived in Nara.

Frank and I were invited to spend the night with a different aunt and uncle, a real treat for us. When we put on our pajamas, Susan pulled out the Cootie game, and we played for nearly forty-five minutes. Cootie is a board game in which players take turns throwing dice to add the cootie's legs and feelers to the body. The first one with a completed bug wins the game. My aunt made some hot pimento-cheese dip, which we ate with large Fritos, washing it down with large glasses of ice-cold Coke while we watched the late movie on TV. We played Parcheesi for a while before climbing into bed. My older cousin, Anna, turned the radio on low, and the Everly Brothers sang us to sleep. The next day, my cousins gave me some skirts and blouses they had outgrown. Now I had some stylish new clothes to wear. I felt much loved, and I was delighted with these unexpected gifts. I wondered what Mama-san would think of me in sandals, a peasant blouse, and a full skirt with petticoats.

Frank spent the night with an aunt and uncle who did not have children. They stayed up late at night watching TV. For a snack they made hot chocolate and ate vanilla ice cream covered with chocolate sauce and pecans. While Frank and I were with our relatives, my mother had time to spend alone with her parents and talk about our life in Nara. We stayed in Houston with my grandparents for almost two weeks before heading to Lampasas, where we would live for eighteen months before moving on to yet another assignment.

1. My parents beside our house on Chestnut Street. Our blue Ford is behind them.
2. While we lived in Lampasas, we visited our grandparents in Bellaire often. Frank and I are in the front yard of our grandparents' yard. I was 12 and Frank was 8.
3. My mother and Frank in front of our house on Chestnut Street.
4. My father in front of the drugstore. I dont recognize the car.
5. The Christmas picture I had taken for our parents in 1956.

Lampasas

We arrived in the middle of January after a long drive from Houston in our light-blue 1955 Ford. What would our lives be like in this small town? What promise, if any, did the old house bring to us? Silently, we carted suitcases, paper bags, maps, coats, snacks, books, and Christmas presents into the cold and empty house.

Before we had time to even look around, there was a knock at the front door. My father opened it to find a smiling Mrs. Brandon Smith, who lived catty-corner to us. She asked if we needed any blankets because there was supposed to be a blue norther that night, or if we needed any rags to clean with. It seemed the house had been empty for a while. My mother politely declined, and my father expressed thanks for her thoughtfulness. Satisfied that she had given us a thorough screening, she said, "If y'all need anything at all, just come on over." My parents smiled at this warm welcome to central Texas.

The old one-story house was located on Chestnut Street across from the public school and was surrounded by large oak trees. Mrs. Spivey, our next-door neighbor, had been widowed for some time. She maintained a small vegetable garden in the backyard and always wore a sunbonnet when she was outside. She loved having a family living next door. Her raspy voice gave us a frequent and warm "hello" or "how are y'all doin'?" We rarely locked the doors, and we slept with the windows open in the spring, summer, and fall.

The local Broiler Burger, a hangout for the high-school crowd, was located on the main highway through town and was just behind our house. I couldn't wait for supper to be over every evening so I could stand outside in the backyard and shake the tablecloth free of crumbs while my eyes roamed for any cars or faces I might know. One of my parents would often remind me that we didn't have ten minutes worth of crumbs on the tablecloth and to come inside immediately.

At school I felt invisible to the other seventh-grade students, who wore cowboy boots, tight denim jeans, and cowboy shirts. When the girls weren't wearing jeans, they wore full circular skirts with lots of white petticoats underneath, scoop-necked blouses, ballet flats, and very long hair. Many of the girls were already wearing makeup and lots of it. Most of the boys wore cowboy hats when school was out. It was not unusual to see the boys driving pickups through town after school as well as on Saturday. Almost everyone belonged to the Future Farmers of America. This was my first jolt of adjustment.

I missed being in Japan so much. I kept singing Japanese songs, practicing the alphabet, counting in Japanese, and repeating all the words and phrases I knew. I loved to repeat all of this to my music teacher, who seemed open to friendship until I started using Japanese.

Her eyes just disappeared into her round, wrinkled face that blended into mounds of gray hair piled in a topknot on her small head. Her short, rotund body jiggled like Jello when she shuffled across the room. When she frowned at me while I was singing a Japanese song to her, I was so disappointed. I thought she would be a perfect replacement for Mama-san, who was so kind to me. But then she said, "Those people killed all of our boys," and I had no idea what she was talking about. She certainly didn't know Mama-san or Mr. and Mrs. Kimoto or even Hatsie, but I knew then I couldn't share my longing for Japan with her or anyone else in Lampasas.

The next surprise came during PE. I did not know how to play softball, and none of the girls wanted me on their team. It was so humiliating! I went home for lunch in tears the first week of school. When I confessed this failure to my mother, she said I should tell the teacher and ask her for help.

After my PE teacher heard that I did not know how to play softball, she paired me with another student who played well. My father bought me a softball glove and helped me practice throwing and catching the ball on weekends. In time I learned to control the ball, which meant that after a while I didn't throw it at the car windows or at the house. I'd had much more control over my hands when I took piano lessons in Nara, but I was learning, and eventually the girls started choosing me to be on a team.

When summer came, we were visited by several groups of our relatives. Pallets of blankets and sheets were all over the house for a while. Everyone waited patiently for a turn in our one bathroom. Younger cousins were willing to lie down and take a nap, after a lunch of tuna or bologna and cheese sandwiches on Mrs. Baird's white bread, Dentler Maid potato chips, and iced Coke to wash it down and cool off. Central Texas was in the fifth year of a severe drought, and nothing escaped the unrelenting heat.

My mother became active in St. Mary's Episcopal Church, which was not far from our house. She was especially fond of the minister's wife, Derby Hirst, who was also a native Houstonian. My mother became friends with several other military wives living in Lampasas. Sometimes she played bridge during the day. My father became a Mason and maintained our yard. We drove to Houston to visit my mother's family about once a month. My grandfather barbecued on Sunday and the whole family came for lunch. My mother, as well as my grandparents, were especially happy during these times. In September when school started again, some girls in my class were talking about cheerleading. One of them asked me offhandedly if I would like to try out too. I think it was probably more of a dare, but to me it was an invitation. Tryouts were held in front of the seventh and eighth grades during a morning assembly in the gym. All the teachers and the principal were present. Excitement crackled in the air as prospective cheerleaders were called to the center of the gym floor. After several girls performed, it was finally my turn. I stood silently for just a moment and then my arms gyrated and my hips were swinging. "Boom-A-Lacka! Boom-A-Lacka! Boom! Boom! Boom!" I shouted from the middle of the gym floor. Several other girls performed after me. That afternoon no one was more surprised than I to learn that I had made the six-member squad. I didn't walk around singing Japanese songs to myself any more. I lived in Lampasas now.

The football stadium was about three blocks from our house. On Friday nights, around six o'clock, crowds started walking to the stadium. Some people carried cow-bells to ring when the home team made a touchdown. Most of the girls wore heavy chrysanthemum corsages with tiny bells and lots of ribbons in school colors. After a winning football game, the team, cheerleaders, and everyone in the stadium headed for the town square in cars and pickups to shout, whoop, and honk horns in gratitude for the win. Crepe-paper streamers waved from the lead cars. Messages of team support were written on all the windows with soap. Students spilled out of car windows or the backs of pickups. Some couples, sitting in the back seats, kissed in the lamplight while the procession made several trips around the town square. My mother was always ready to head for home after one trip around, but if I didn't shout too much and wasn't too loud, she would agree to drive around a second time, much to my delight.

My mother only drove around the square when she went grocery shopping at the Piggly Wiggly grocery store on the northwest corner of the square. She always looked for a parallel parking space in front. On Saturdays I usually went with her. One particular Saturday we saw several adults standing in the middle of each block on the square. As we walked toward Piggly Wiggly, we noticed coins laid out in a line all the way down the block. The lady standing in the middle of the block approached us and asked if we would like to give some money to the March of Dimes. The local chapter was trying to raise enough money to stretch all the way around the square. My mother opened her purse, took out all of her change, and handed it over to the lady who was delighted and thanked her again and again. The March of Dimes was founded to support research for a cure for polio, which was still an epidemic at that time. Maybe they could help my cousin in Houston who was afflicted with polio before we left for Japan in 1952.

Much to my surprise I was invited to spend the night with Judy, the most popular girl in the seventh grade. Her parents were older than other middle-school parents. Her father owned a local business, and they lived in a very nice home. Judy had a beautiful bedroom with a canopied bed and her own bathroom. She wore very stylish clothes from Miller's Department Store, the best place to shop for nice clothes in Lampasas. Did this invitation mean that I had finally been accepted by local people as one of their own?

I loved everything Judy had, everything she wore, and everything she ate. When my mother arrived to pick me up I had not finished eating the cinnamon toast Mrs. Scott prepared for breakfast because every time she asked me if I would like some more I said, "Yes, ma'am. This is delicious. I certainly would." So I was still eating my fourth piece of cinnamon toast and drinking my fourth cup of hot chocolate when it was time to go home.

I insisted on showing my mother everything in Judy's room and all the clothes she and I had looked at the night before. I was still in disbelief when I showed my mother her lovely bathroom and her beautiful bedroom, not realizing how embarrassing this might be for my mother. When we finally got in the car, she only said that I didn't have to be so enthusiastic about everything Judy owned.

Other invitations followed Judy's, including one from Mabel, who had red hair and lived in the country. She was giving a Halloween party for the entire seventh grade. I was excited and frightened. Did I really want to go to this party with people I didn't know very well? I wasn't sure what to expect. I didn't know what would be expected of me, but I was equally afraid not to go.

The girls, who were dressed in tight jeans, makeup, and cologne, clustered at one end of the food table; the boys, in tight jeans, after-shave lotion, and cowboy boots or tennis shoes, clustered at the other end. Neither group acknowledged that the other group was present. Hot dogs, popcorn, cookies, and candy corn covered the table, which was set up between two trees.

Soon Mabel said loudly, "Okay, everybody, let's play Seven Up!" We played for a short time, and then one of the girls grabbed Lew Miller, whose parents' owned Miller's Department Store, and yelled, "Everybody line up and kiss Lewwww!" Two girls, one on either side, held one of his arms tightly. The girls quickly lined up behind Mable and, one by one, tauntingly walked or skipped up to Lew and planted a kiss on his lips or on his cheeks. His face was soon covered in lipstick. Lew stood helplessly between the two girls, his knees bent and his head lowered. Sometimes his eyes were closed. Sometimes he had a smile on his face. But he blushed through the entire ordeal.

"Has everybody kissed Lew?" Mabel yelled. There was silence except for some giggling. Mabel looked around,

"Mary Lou, have you kissed Lew, yet?"

"No," I replied, quietly horrified.

"Hurry up, and get over here!" she yelled.

I walked quickly toward Lew and brushed my lips to his soft cheek while he looked down at his tennis shoes. I wished my mother would come and pick me up.

I loved being a cheerleader, and I especially loved the fanfare cheerleaders got at our football games. I never stopped smiling, except in math class. I had lots of friends. Sometimes I would stay after school and talk with my English teacher, who was fun to be with. I wanted to live in Lampasas forever.

A Trip to Blytheville, Arkansas

While we lived in Lampasas, my father's family gathered at his mother's home in Blytheville, Arkansas, for a family reunion. Her five children and all the grandchildren came from Detroit, Michigan; Tracy, California; Lampasas, Texas; and St. James, Missouri.

My cousin, Helen, who lived with Grandma, was fourteen, and I was twelve. She was my constant companion. She taught me how to sew two bandanas into a blouse, how to twirl a baton, and how to pop popcorn on a wood-burning stove. We giggled and talked under the quilts my grandmother made by hand and stuffed with field cotton long after everyone else had gone to sleep. Wearing short shorts, we used to stand in front of the old mirrored armoire and examine our legs for maturity, tone, and beauty—characteristics I didn't know I was supposed to have. Wearing our bandana shirts, we looked at our breasts in the mirror. We stood up straight and threw our shoulders back, trying to make ourselves look larger than we were. I felt inadequate because Helen was so far ahead of me, physically and emotionally. She lived a faster life than I did, and I was fascinated.

My uncle, who lived next door, delivered blocks of ice to businesses and residents who had an ice-box type of refrigerator. My aunt was a wonderful cook and did catering for the large Baptist church in Blytheville. She invited us for lunch, the biggest meal of the day, and my mother and I went over to help her. Early that morning, she'd gathered an armload of fresh corn on the cob from her large garden in the back of the house and deposited it in the kitchen sink. When I looked in the sink, I asked her what was coming out of the top of the corn. She replied that it was silk. I asked if I could touch it. "You've never seen fresh corn on the cob?" she asked in surprise. "No, ma'am," I answered. She dropped the fresh radishes she was carrying on the kitchen table, went to the sink, picked up an ear of corn, and pulled the husks back so I could feel the silk and the corn. I was fascinated. Of course, the silk didn't look like the silk fabric my mother used to sew, but it did have a silky feeling, and I couldn't wait to taste the cooked fresh corn on the cob.

Another time Helen and I sat on the back steps of my grandmother's house, talking while my grandmother quietly hulled peas into a large washtub. After a few minutes, Helen took me to the backyard and began to point out the squash blossoms, telling me they were going to be squash. Then she showed me the watermelons growing on a vine near the fence. She started thumping them one at a time, instructing me to listen to the different sounds each one made when she "thumped" them.

"Listen," she said, "do you hear that?"

"Yes," I answered shyly. No one had ever given me such details about vegetables and fruit.

"This one is ripe." She thumped it again. "Hear how it sounds when you thump it in the middle? Now you try it."

I thumped it and heard the correct sound. She instructed me to thump another one and tell her if it was ripe or not. I thumped the next watermelon, but the sound was different.

"This one is not ripe," I reported.

"Good!" she exclaimed, pleased with my progress. She ran back to my grandmother and reported that I had learned to recognize squash blossoms and could tell if a watermelon was ripe.

My grandmother nodded her approval. We sat down on the concrete steps again.

"Have you ever put beans up your nose?" Helen asked me suddenly.

"No," I said cautiously.

"Well, if you choose small ones, you can sniff them right up and then blow them out. It's easy. I'll show you." With her left hand, she took several small peas out of the washtub my grandmother was using. She took one, held her head back, put the pea at the base of her nose, and sniffed loudly.

"Look," she said, "do you see the pea when you look at me?"

"No," I answered surprised. She blew it out and then tried the same experiment with two peas, one in each nostril. After she blew out both of the peas, she said, "Okay, it's your turn now. Here are the peas." She put two small peas in my hand. I sat there, staring at the peas.

"Hurry up," Helen said. "we're going inside to eat in a minute." I held my head back and put a pea at the base of my nose and tried to sniff, but nothing happened.

"Try it again," she said. I repeated the same posture and sniffed harder. This time I had success, but I couldn't blow the pea out of my nose no matter how hard I tried. I was going to try and pick it out, but Helen was horrified.

"Don't pick it!" she yelled. "You'll just push it up farther and it will never come out! It'll grow, and you'll have a vine coming out of your nose!" I was scared to death. I thought about going to school and having to tell every teacher why a vine was growing out of my nose. Helen prevailed on my grandmother for help.

"Go inside and bring me that long needle on my pin cushion," my grandmother said quietly. "Take the thread out of it." I panicked, and my breathing came faster and harder. I couldn't imagine what my grandmother was going to do with a large needle, but I was finding it difficult to breathe. I wished I could be some other place.

Helen returned with the needle. My grandmother calmly removed the washtub full of peas from her lap and put it on the steps. She told me to come and stand in front of her and not to be afraid. "Be very still now," she said calmly as she held my arm and pushed the needle up into my nostril. She flicked her wrist and the pea popped out. I could breathe again.

"There," she said, "you girls don't put any more peas up your noses now, hear?"

"Yes, ma'am," we answered together.

In the evening we played chase, caught lightning bugs, and tried to evade mosquitoes. The adults sat in lawn chairs on my grandmother's front lawn and talked. My father's brothers and sisters were great storytellers. There was so much laughter among the adults. Sometimes my cousin and I would sit in the grass and just listen to them talking and laughing. The next minute, we were up catching lightning bugs, putting them in mason jars, watching their lights go on and off.

My mother and father went off on an errand one morning and took my aunt with them. Our cousin Alan was in charge of Frank, Helen, and me. Alan had bright red hair and freckles. He was still in high school and was lots of fun to be with because he made jokes out of any situation. He could also wiggle his ears back and forth and up and down. Frank and I couldn't believe our eyes when we watched him. Neither of us could move our ears, no matter how hard we tried. Everyone loved Alan, but Frank wasn't so sure he wanted to stay without my parents around. As my father backed out of the driveway, Frank ran after the car. Alan convinced him to stay in the yard with us by moving his ears and not moving his facial muscles. Frank was spellbound.

While Frank was still at ease, Alan went to the garage and came back with a long piece of thick rope. I froze in my tracks. Why did he need a long, thick rope? Alan told Frank to stand in front of the large oak tree by the front porch. He began to wrap the rope around Frank and the tree. My brother could still move, but he couldn't get away from the tree. Helen and I sat on the grass while Alan sat on the concrete steps. We watched as Frank tried to get loose from the rope. Alan entertained us with stories and jokes. Frank joined us in laughter and forgot about being tied up.

When my parents came back, they stared through the windshield at Frank tied to the tree. Alan told them he was afraid Frank would run away. My parents got out of the car in a good humor. My father went over to the tree, untied and unwound the rope, and Frank took off for the backyard.

On another day, my cousin Helen and I walked to town. She was going to show me all the best places in downtown Blytheville and the places my uncle delivered large blocks of ice. It seemed like a great adventure to me. Helen talked all the way to town. We crossed the railroad track while I tried my best to listen to everything she said, taking in the old buildings, the traffic on the brick streets, and the clothes people were wearing. I was ready to go back to my grandmother's house, but she kept walking and talking from one business to another. We ran into my uncle delivering ice at three places. Finally, a train whistle blew in the distance.

"Come on," she said. "Let's run across the train track in front of the engine!"

"No!" I said horrified. The engine moved closer to us, and the engineer blew the warning horn.

"Don't be chicken," she said.

"What if the train doesn't stop?" I asked. The engine approached, and the horn was blowing continuously.

"He doesn't stop," she said. "That's the idea. You run across the tracks while the engineer is picking up speed. I do it all the time, and I haven't been hit yet." She smiled and tossed her thick blonde curls.

I was too frightened to answer. I didn't want to run in front of a moving train, and I didn't want to watch my cousin get hit. The engineer must have seen us wavering close to the track because the horn blew loudly and constantly. I could feel the wind generated by the moving train, trying to pull us into the engine.

"Come on!" she yelled. I opened my mouth as she ran directly in front of the engine. I stood with my hands over my mouth, looking at the the redfaced engineer, and the train rattling in front of me, the wind trying to pull me under the wheels. It was a long freight train, and I thought it would never end, but finally the caboose passed. There was Helen standing with her hand on her hip, shaking her thick blonde curls, smiling at me with self-satisfaction.

"Why didn't you run?" she said, staring me in the eyes.

"I didn't want to," I said.

"Why not?" she said.

"I just didn't want to," I said, looking down at the rocks by the side of the tracks.

We headed back to my grandmother's house. It was time for lunch. I was hungry, thirsty, and scared out of my mind. Helen talked all the way back to our grandmother's house.

Before we left Blytheville, my grandmother prepared a special midday meal for all of us. Twenty people crowded around the table in her small dining room. She was not used to cooking for so many people at one time, and it was after one o'clock before we all sat down. I was very hungry and had been for some time. Helen sat next to my mother, and I sat across from both of them. My father sat at the head of the table. No one could remember the last time all my grandmother's children and grandchildren had sat down together for one of her home-cooked meals.

When we left, my grandmother loaded our car trunk with preserved and pickled vegetables that she'd picked and put up herself. That delighted my parents, especially my mother.

Transition

When we returned to Lampasas, I proudly wore my new blouse made of two dark-blue bandanas stitched together at the shoulders and under the arms. I practiced twirling my baton wearing short shorts and sandals in the backyard every chance I could get. My eyes always roamed the Broiler Burger parking lot for familiar cars and faces, hoping that someone would notice me the way I was noticing them.

I imagined how I would look in a twirler's uniform at a Friday night football game. The crowd not only would cheer loudly, they would stand up when I pranced onto the field, shaking white plumes on top of my head while spinning a splendid new baton at arm's length like a top. I threw my twirling baton high into the air but missed it, and it crashed onto the concrete patio. Darn it! There was a big dent near the top, but I picked it up and kept practicing. Eventually I found myself in band class as a majorette who frequently dropped her baton.

I never marched with the band at a football game, but I remember marching around the school leading the band and coming to a complete halt in front of our house, which was across from the school. As I shouted the band through several simple formations, my parents came outside and watched proudly before we marched on. I felt so important when they smiled at me.

For my thirteenth birthday, my parents let me have me a skating party at the local National Guard Armory. This was a popular place for junior-high-school birthday parties. I was thrilled to celebrate my birthday like everyone else in junior high and invited everyone in my homeroom. We brought our own skates and skated in a big circle to popular music. Halfway through the two-hour party, we stopped for hot dogs, chips, and Cokes. My mother had a sheet cake made at the local bakery. Everyone sang "Happy Birthday," and I blew out the candles. I tried to cut the cake, but my mother finished cutting it and served it on the paper plates I picked out at Piggly Wiggly. It was exciting and scary at the same time. I had only been to one skating party, and I hoped I was doing everything the right way. My father and Frank were there too. I felt very important even though my father didn't smile all evening.

I loved living in Lampasas. I had lots of friends. I was a cheerleader, and I made good grades. Everyone knew me. I was confirmed at St. Mary's Episcopal Church. When I was home sick with a cold once, a group of students I knew walked by my house, calling my name. Someone even threw a handful of small rocks on the roof, which had my mother outside immediately.

"Don't throw rocks on our roof," she said with a smile.

"Okay," they said. "We just came by to see Mary Lou."

"She's sick," my mother said. "She can't come outside."

"When is she coming back?"

"In a few days," my mother said. "Don't throw rocks on the roof anymore," and she came inside.

When I heard voices I opened my bedroom window so I could hear and see who was asking about me. The students saw me in the window as they moved toward the Broiler Burger behind our house.

"Hey, what's wrong with you?" someone asked.

"I'm sick," I said, sounding like my nose was stuffed with cotton.

"Yeah, you sound sick. Do you live here?"

"Yeah, this is my house."

"Are you coming back to school?" someone asked.

"Yeah. I have to get well first. How was Mr. Bellamy's class today?"

"Oh, it was okay. We didn't do nothin'.'"

This sounded good to me because I didn't like Mr. Bellamy's math class. My mother had to help me with the word problems, which I hated. When another girl and I had finished our homework and no one else had, he let the two of us polish the broad green leaves on his plants and go the girls' restroom to get water in his watering can. We walked around the room, cleaning chalk dust off the leaves and watering his plants while he explained the homework one more time to the other students. Lucky for me that my mother was good at word problems.

"I have to go now."

"Bye, Mary Lou. Get well."

I closed the window as they headed slowly toward the Broiler Burger to get Cokes and fries. I wished I could go with them, but my parents did not allow me to do this. I felt that I had a place among the students in Lampasas. They made me feel that I belonged there. I felt that Lampasas was my home.

In the fall of 1956, we watched television reports of the Hungarian uprising with interest since my father was headed for Munich, Germany, in January. We would follow when housing was available. *Moving again. Starting all over again. Another new school. Maybe new friends. Maybe not. What would it be like this time? I was saddened by this change in our future, but no one knew that I was relieved to be away from the pressure of having to date in the eighth grade.*

In retrospect, I wonder if my father reflected on his first trip to Europe as a twenty-two-year-old going to war in southern England. He'd left Camp Kilmer, New Jersey, in November 1943 on the *Capetown Castle*, the sixth-largest ship in the British Merchant Marine. It was built for eight hundred men but was overloaded with three thousand young men, all going to the war in Europe. He was assigned to quarters in the bottom of the ship and had to share his bunk with someone else, so he slept on the deck. There were only two meals a day and a cold shower once a week for three weeks. On December 5, 1943, he wrote in his diary: "I was really glad I talked with Sara before I left. God bless her and Mary Lou. I still love her more than I know how to say. But I'll be back some day! And we will start life all over again and be happy forever." There hadn't been time for him to see his mother before he left.

In December he took Frank and drove to Blytheville to bring his mother and niece, Helen, to spend Christmas week with us in Lampasas. Before they left I took Frank to a photography studio in downtown Lampasas and had our picture taken professionally as a present to our parents. My parents were very surprised and loved the picture. Grandma and Helen had never been away for Christmas. We showed them around the square in downtown Lampasas and showed them the Christmas decorations in the surrounding area, but mostly we stayed at home and enjoyed being together. Helen and I played cards, and sometimes Frank joined us in board games while my parents talked with Grandma.

In the middle of January I came home for lunch as usual, but this was the day my father was leaving for Munich. He was standing in the living room with his hands on his hips. His green eyes glared at me; his face was steeled in a stern look. I was afraid to approach him. I stood staring for a moment and then said quietly, "Good-bye, Daddy." He responded with an "Okay," and a nod of his head. His facial muscles relaxed, and a smile crept into the corner of his lips. My mother frowned at him. I walked out of the front door, closing it quietly behind me. Before I reached the end of the sidewalk, sobs overtook me. At the same time the door opened suddenly, and my mother gently called to me, telling me to come back inside and say good-bye. Silently, I wiped my eyes and my nose and reentered the house. My mother must have scolded him because he laughed as he put his arms around me and patted me on the back. He said that everything would be all right, and that I was to do a good job. I was the oldest, and I knew that more was expected of me.

I walked quietly outside one more time and stood on the sidewalk sobbing, not knowing which way to turn. Mrs. Spivey's raspy voice called me from her front porch to come over. She hugged me for a while and then took me inside to sit down, speaking gently all the while. Eventually, embarrassment crept over me, and I returned to school. I was tardy and went to the office crying quietly and was offered a chair, where I spent the afternoon.

Living in Lampasas was the closest we ever came to living a stable American life. Each of us had wonderful friends. My mother was active in the Episcopal Church. Frank had school friends his age to play with. My father was more relaxed while we lived in Lampasas and even became a mason, but with his departure, the stability that Lampasas represented disappeared. It was hard for all of us to leave, but new adventures were waiting on the horizon.

1. Frank and I during the first day on board the ship heading for Bremerhaven, Germany, March 1957.
2. My father in Munich, Germany, 1957-1959

Atlantic Bound

Thick fog shrouded the harbor as we headed out of New York into the Atlantic, making our late afternoon departure seem more like evening. I could see only the outline of the Statue of Liberty as we passed, but when I did emotions hit me hard. We were going to the heart and homeland of WWII. What lay ahead for us? Were there any remnants of the war years left? How would we be regarded by the German people? None of us knew what to expect. Most of the families on board the MSTS ship were women and children heading to Europe to join their husbands and fathers stationed there. I anticipated a pleasant trip, but as soon as I boarded the ship and smelled the diesel fuel, I was seasick.

We were subjected to lifeboat drills again, just as we had been on our trip to and from Japan. Every day at the same time, we put on our lifejackets and headed to our designated area on deck to answer roll call. We stood still and quiet in the same order every day while crew members lowered the lifeboats into the choppy Atlantic. Sometimes a crew member would take one of the lifeboats out into the ocean, making a large circle near the boat. It returned to the ship, and the lifeboats were pulled back up above the decks and secured for another timed drill. We were certain that we would not have to abandon ship, but the drills gave us a sense of security in the event of an emergency—though they also gave us a feeling of anxiety.

After we had been at sea for about a week, my mother encouraged me to go out on deck and get some fresh air. I had been feeling queasy that morning, but not seasick. I went out on the deck, holding tightly to the railing and watched the water from the horizon to the side of the ship. It was overcast, and the wind was blowing. I loved the feel of the wind blowing through my hair. The water was choppy, but the ship was cutting through the water at a steady speed. We had been at sea for about seven days and were entering the English Channel. I stood holding on to the rail for a moment longer. There was no sign of land or even seagulls.

I started climbing the steep, narrow, metal stairs that connected one deck to the next when more people came out on the main deck. I didn't want to answer questions about where I was going to live in Germany or where I was coming from in the States. I looked for empty deck chairs as I approached each deck. The higher I climbed, the fewer and fewer people there were about, and after four flights of stairs, I spotted two deck chairs near the large, double smokestacks on the top deck. A middle-aged woman in dark sunglasses was lying on one, covered with a blanket. I lay down in the other and looked away from her. The air was crisp, and the wind was still blowing hard. It felt good to lie down on the open deck with a few warm sun rays on my face. Maybe I would get over the seasickness. I reflected on the life I left behind in Lampasas, my grandparents, and my cousins. I wondered if we really would see them all again, if my grandparents would still be living when we returned. Mostly, I wondered what our life in Munich would be like.

Suddenly the ship lurched. The woman and I were thrown hard into the metal railing of the deck. When I opened my eyes, the woman was racing down the stairs. I held on, afraid to move in case the ship lurched again. After a minute or two, I stood up slowly, holding onto the rail to steady myself. My right hip and shin hurt. My right arm and shoulder felt sore and bruised, but I had to get to my mother and brother.

I made my way slowly down the stairs, holding onto the hand rail with both hands. I was very worried about my mother and Frank. I moved down the steep metal stairs to the main deck, one step at a time, entered the salon, and headed down the hallway to our stateroom, holding onto the rail. Bob, the old steward who cleaned our room and made the beds every day, was standing with his arm on my mother's shoulder. She was crying quietly and holding on to the bedpost. I stood in the doorway staring at them for a moment, worried that something had happened to my mother.

"She was worried about you," Bob said quietly, looking down at the floor as he left the room.

I told her how I had been thrown from the deck chair into the railing on the top deck when the ship had lurched. I was sore and bruised on the right side where I had hit the railing, but I was all right. I explained that the woman next to me had been thrown too, but she had run down the stairs immediately. I asked about Frank, and I wanted to know what had caused the lurch. My mother told me Frank was playing a board game with a little boy in a cabin three doors down from ours. Bob told my mother the lurch was probably an underground tidal wave. I stayed with my mother for a while, reading on the bunk bed until she collected herself. After a few minutes, she missed Frank, so we walked together to the cabin where he was playing, and then we walked on deck with her.

While we were walking around on deck, I met a blonde-headed teenager with a long pony tail and beautiful green eyes walking with her mother. Her easy smile drew me to her. When I introduced myself, we were both surprised to learn that Barbara and her family were headed to Munich. We had so much to share and so many questions to ask. We didn't know it at the time, but we would meet again at Munich American High School, where we would have some classes together.

After a few more days in rough waters of the English Channel, we arrived in Bremerhaven on a cold, dark, overcast day. From the main deck we could see huge cranes moving goods from the hold to the docks, not only from our ship, but from countless other ships in port. Excited about getting off the ship, yet anxious about the next leg of the trip, we packed last-minute items, put our luggage outside the cabin door, and said good-bye to our steward, Bob, who had been so kind to us. Passenger hand luggage on board would be transported to the dock on large dollies. From Bremerhaven, we would ride a train to Frankfurt where my father would meet us.

The train ride was our first experience in Germany. We were in a compartment, and my mother seemed more relaxed now. She allowed me to walk through our railcar and speak with other people who had been on the ship with us. Frank spent most of his day looking out of the window at the passing landscape and reading. Our arrival in Germany was unlike our arrival in Japan, where we easily stood out because of our appearance and because there were so few Americans in Japan at that time. My mother took note of this. "I don't feel that we are really in a foreign country at all because we look just like the Germans. The only thing separating us is the language," she said.

I do not ever remember ever seeing my parents so happy to see each other as when we arrived at the large Bahnhoff (train station) in Frankfurt. My father gave Frank and me each a big hug while saying how good we looked and how glad he was to see us. After we collected all of our luggage, he picked up two suitcases and headed for the exit. Frank and I followed closely behind our parents to the army sedan. My father introduced us to the driver, a young soldier who worked with him at McGraw Kasern (command post). Together they loaded our luggage into the back of the sedan, and we were on our way to Munich. We had to make several stops on the way because I was carsick. In between stops I tried to sleep.

On the outskirts of Munich, we passed city blocks with mountains of loose soil. Jagged edges of concrete, broken pieces of wood, thick pieces of steel bent in odd shapes, and unrecognizable pieces of construction materials protruded from the soil.

"Daddy," Frank said, "what is that? What are those dirt mountains for?"

"Oh, that's just rubble and debris from bombings during the war," he said in an offhand sort of way, as if it were nothing unusual.

I wondered what kind of place this was, what really happened here, and if we would live near anything like the mountains of debris. As we drove further into the city, it was clear that there had been a lot of bombing. We passed blocks with only the shells of buildings remaining—no roofs, windows, or doors. There were once fine old building facades, some still with faded pictures on the front. Many of the empty buildings had deep pock marks from bullets or explosions. All the rubble and debris had been removed. I wondered what it must have been like for people living in the now deserted buildings when the bombs fell. I wondered what stories the walls could tell. A thick silence settled in the car as we drove through the city. Frank stared out of the windows. I wasn't sure I wanted to live here at all. My mother's face was tense, my father's face clouded over. The driver, his eyebrows knitted together, stared straight through the front windshield.

When we arrived at the hotel in downtown Munich, custodians unloaded our luggage. We were excited about ending our long trip in such a nice place. Mostly it was a relief that we didn't have to travel any more. I was still dizzy and couldn't wait to lie down. We had been traveling for a month. I had been seasick and unable to hold anything in my stomach while we were at sea. The motion sickness and dizziness stayed with me while we drove from Frankfurt to Munich. I slept soundly for two days and one night without waking. When I did wake up, my mother and father took turns spoon-feeding me warm, delicious oxtail broth. They kept a close watch on me, making sure that I ate something at every meal.

Our last evening in the hotel, we went downstairs for dinner in the restaurant. Large old prints on the wall showed pictures of early Munich. While my father explained that we were living in a city eight hundred years old, a stringed trio on a small stage tuned their instruments and began to play Strauss waltzes as we ate. I was enchanted, and I couldn't stop staring at the musicians, the art on the walls, and the people sitting near us in the small restaurant. Maybe we did look just like the German people, but this was definitely different than living in the States. In the morning, we moved to our apartment in Perlacher Forst, where we would live for two years and nine months, longer than any place we had lived before.

1. Mr. Gruckenberg, Helga, his daughter, and I swimming at Chiemsee near Munich. I was fifteen here.
2. Frank and I playing in the snow behind our apartment in Munich.

Munich, Germany

Evening light poured into a quiet room through a wide picture window in the middle of the wall. Warm light glowed in the windows of the apartments across the street. Cars filled the parking lots in front of the gray apartment buildings. Large, black numerals identified each building. A few stars appeared in the night sky. A thin layer of ice reflected the yellow light of the street lamps as a few pedestrians moved toward unknown destinations, the sound of their boots marking the passage of time on the sidewalks.

A thin ribbon of cigarette smoke spiraled slowly up from the desk toward the ceiling and snaked silently around the sparsely furnished living room. My father, absorbed in a book, sat stone-faced and tense in a wooden chair in front of a large oak desk with neatly stacked papers. In his left hand, he held the remains of a Camel cigarette over a glass ashtray filled with ashes; in his right hand he held an open book. His eyes moved quickly across the open pages. My mother sat quietly on the sofa, reading a thick book. Her tall, slender body, erect and tense, sat motionless as she turned the pages. My father inhaled from the stub of a Camel cigarette and crushed the remaining embers with one finger, moving the wooden chair slightly. My mother looked up, disturbed by the squeaking movement of the chair, then lowered her head and continued to read. It was March 1957. I was thirteen and Frank was nine.

A knock on the front door alerted the attention of both my parents. Frank came from the hallway and opened the door to find an old woman holding a large basket filled with bundles of fresh flowers. "Bitte schoen, Jungen, wuerdest du etwas blumen?" (Young man, would you like some flowers?), she asked.

She smiled broadly and offered him a small bouquet of bright yellow flowers. "Funf mark" (five marks), she continued, smiling. My mother walked to the door, smiled, remarked on the beauty of the flowers, and answered, "No, thank you." She pushed the door, but the old woman persisted, "Nur drei mark, jetzt" (Only three marks now). My mother repeated, "No, thank you," and to Frank's relief, closed the door.

"Good," my father said. "Testing you about buying goods from the Germans." He returned to his book. My mother walked into the kitchen; Frank followed close behind. She pulled out an apron and tied the strings in back as I came in. I got some placemats, napkins, and silverware and then set the table. Frank stood in the kitchen, watching my mother.

"Mr. and Mrs. Gruckenberg have invited us to their home tomorrow," my mother said. They've asked us to come in the afternoon, but we'll stay for supper."

"Do they speak English?" I asked.

"No, but their daughter, Helga, does, and so does her husband, Gerhard," she replied.

"Will they have french fries?" Frank asked.

"No," I said, "this is Germany, not France.

The next day we drove through heavy traffic across Munich to meet our new friends. Mr. Gruckenberg and his son-in-law, Gerhard, were waiting outside to greet us. Extending his hand, Gerhard helped my mother out of the car and then shook hands with my father, Frank, and me.

Upstairs in the small apartment, Mrs. Gruckenberg and Helga were waiting to greet us. Like her husband, Mrs. Gruckenberg was short, but stout. Helga, about twenty, was short and very attractive with large blue eyes and curly dark hair. Gerhard, her tall, handsome husband, was in his late twenties, with large blue eyes and blond hair. He worked for BMW – engines (BMW Triebwerke constructed engines for airplanes) in Munich-Allach. We were invited to sit on covered benches and chairs around a small table. Coffee and tea were offered to my parents, Coke and juice to Frank and me. For a while we sat quietly, taking in the small, neat space of what was once part of a larger room.

White lace curtains framed a small window; tiny pink flowers covered the creamy wallpaper. Old family pictures in dark wooden frames sat on top of a table by the sofa. A bookshelf next to the doorframe was filled with old books in leather covers; on top was a piece of lace and more family pictures. A metal floor lamp with a cream-colored shade stood next to the sofa. Several landscape watercolors hung on the walls.

My father and his friend Jon Madsen, a Danish Lieutenant, went to a Faschingsball at the Lowenbraeukeller in February 1957 before my mother, Frank, and I arrived in Munich. The Gruckenbergs were there as well with Helga and her fiancée, Gerhard. As he was very interested in Americans, Gerhard started a conversation. My father invited them for bingo at McGraw Kaserne, where my father worked. My mother, Frank, and I met the Gruckenberg family for the first time at their home. The next year my mother went with my father to the Fasching Ball, a pre-Lenten festival.

In the spring of 1958 we attended Helga and Gerhard's beautiful wedding at the Lutherkirke in Giesing, and the reception in the Café am Zoo where we met their whole family. It was a wonderful event.

Mrs. Gruckenberg came in with a box of chocolate candy and offered it to Frank, who took two pieces, and then to me, but I politely refused. Mr. Gruckenberg poured coffee for my parents, while Helga brought in another plate with a variety of cookies. Seated around the small coffee table, they discussed family matters and the nice apartment. This family reminded me of my grandparents in Houston. At the time, I did not know that my maternal great-grandparents had come from Darmstadt.

Frank was fidgety and pulled a small metal car out of his pocket. He rolled it up and down on his pants leg and then moved it to the sofa. My father told him quietly not to put the car on the sofa, but Mr. and Mrs. Gruckenberg admonished my father, encouraging Frank to play with the car. Frank smiled at this endorsement.

Conversation about the apartment led Mr. Gruckenberg, a Schlossermeister, locksmith, to mention he had his own business downstairs. They talked a little about life in Munich during the war years. Mr. Gruckenberg said that after WW I inflation was so bad it was hard to find food. A wheelbarrow full of one-hundred-mark notes would hardly buy a loaf of bread. Later, he told us that he was not a Nazi, but people often had no choice. For example, a camera was set up near a picture of Adolf Hitler in the park. Anyone who passed the picture was required to salute the Fuehrer. Some people walked around the picture to avoid saluting, but the camera took a picture of all persons who did so. The police looked them up, arrested them, and sent them off to a death camp. It was especially difficult during the last years of the war because of the bombs. It was hard to find food and keep warm.

Gerhard leaned forward in his chair and began to talk. "My father was born in 1884, and was an officer in two world wars. At the end of WWII he became a colonel in the Wehrmacht. We moved often within Germany which is the military custom. I could only rarely be with my father because, as a soldier, he was often away.

Because of the air raids during the war, families had been evacuated from Munich. My mother, my two sisters, and I had been evacuated to Garmisch. After the war, my father came to see us for a couple of weeks before he had to go back to Munich to work and look after the apartment. He took his bike because there was no public transportation available. Near Weilheim he was stopped by a very friendly American GI. The GI stopped a truck that had been confiscated by the US Army and asked the driver to take my father with his bike. Near Starnberg the truck collided with another truck and my father was severely injured. On June 23rd 1945, my father died in the hospital in Starnberg.

After an uncomfortable silence, my father began to talk about his experience in England during the war, much to our surprise. Frank and I had never heard him talk about his wartime experiences. A young engineer, my father had spent two years in England building roads and drainage ditches during bitterly cold and rainy winters in hip-deep mud. He had driven all over

England and Wales securing materials for the American camps and had narrowly missed being hit in several bombing raids. After the invasion, he had been sent to school in Paris. When my father became quiet again he told us how he had been notified that his father had died of cancer while he was in England, three weeks after his father had died. We sat in silence for a few minutes, and then Mrs. Gruckenberg and Helga quickly cleared the small table and returned to the kitchen to prepare supper. Offers of help from my mother and me were politely refused, but an uncomfortable silence continued. With talk of the war, horrible memories resurfaced. My father's long face told us he was in terrible place. The faces of the Gruckenberg family revealed that the war years had been cruel to them.

Soon platters of cold cuts came out of the kitchen with baskets of fresh bread. Homemade mayonnaise and several kinds of mustard appeared along with Loewenbrau beer and Coca-Cola. Next, came a large bowl of German potato salad. We wondered how so much food could come out of such a small kitchen, but Helga warned us to save room for strudel.

Both families ate heartily and laughed when Frank made a mustard and mayonnaise sandwich with the car in the middle. I talked about my German studies, and the Gruckenberg family was pleased that I was learning to speak German. My parents invited our hosts to come for dinner in a few weeks. Finally, it was time to go. Hugs and handshakes between all of us went around the room. We left with the satisfaction and happiness that come from being with one's family.

Our evening with the Gruckenberg family was similar to the dinner my parents had had in Nara with Mr. and Mrs. Kimoto when an important historical exchange occurred. This time Frank and I were present to witness the emotional exchange of historical information. Thirteen years after the war, my father, Mr. and Mrs. Gruckenberg, Helga, and Gerhard sat across from each other as friends, sharing a meal and talking about the war.

Before we arrived in Munich, Mr. Gruckenberg introduced my father to Jon Madsen, a Danish army officer and engineer. Jon and my father were good friends, and he came to see us often. My father was very relaxed with Jon; they laughed and talked easily. Sometimes he brought other Danish officer friends with him for dinner at our apartment. Our first summer in Munich, we drove to the World's Fair in Brussels and then to Copenhagen to meet his family. It was a delightful time being in his parents' apartment with his two sisters and brother-in-law. Only Jon and his older sister spoke English. His mother prepared a dinner with wonderful foods that covered the entire dining room table. When he came to stay with us, Jon often took Frank to the Deutsches Museum on the Isar River and helped me with my German homework because he was also fluent in German.

In Munich my mother belonged to the Officers' Wives Club and usually attended monthly luncheons, as she had done in Japan, and sometimes she would consult me about her dress. Periodically, she played bridge with other women in Perlacher Forst during the day, once or twice a month. She also did a lot of sewing, because she made all of my clothes and all of her clothes too.

Eating out in Munich, we discovered good German foods. Wiener schnitzel, red cabbage, sauerkraut, so many kinds of potatoes, oxtail soup, spaetzle (a noodle dish), bratwurst, knackwurst, wonderful sausage, strudel, and anything made with mocha were foods we really enjoyed. Jon Madsen took us to a nice restaurant in downtown Munich not long after we arrived. In the late afternoon, it was filled with people, but we were directed to a table in the middle of the room. Menus were passed around, and we sat pretending to read each item while Jon patiently translated for us. Suddenly I jumped and dropped my menu. Something very cold touched my leg and then touched me again. I jumped again and was about to scream when I moved the white tablecloth and looked under the table into the face of an interested, sniffing dachshund. I was aghast. How did this dog get into the restaurant filled with people? I could see his leash dragging on the floor.

"Schatzie!" someone shouted. Obediently, the dog turned and went under the adjacent table while everyone there tried to hide their obvious amusement. I was burning with embarrassment and picked up my menu.

"People take their dogs out to eat with them here," Jon explained. "It's okay to take your dog into a restaurant."

"It is?" Frank asked, wide-eyed. "You can't do that in Texas."

A row of small restaurants and a bakery were within walking distance of our apartment. Once in a while, I walked to the bakery and, with my babysitting money, bought a piece of mocha layer cake with thick mocha frosting between each layer and piled generously on top. I loved to sit alone under the trees that grew in front of Perlacher Forst, relishing every bite, while reflecting on my life in Munich. I missed my grandparents very much, but there was so much to absorb in Munich.

From our balcony on the back of the apartment, we sometimes noticed a group of nuns sitting and eating in a clearing of the thick forest across the main road behind our apartment building. They wore long black robes and large, stiff, white head coverings that looked like wings. My father had sternly warned us never to cross the heavily traveled road, but after watching the nuns carefully, I decided it couldn't be too dangerous in the forest. Several times, I wandered across the road and just sat in the trees listening to the wind blowing through the pine needles. I always wanted to walk deep into the forest and explore, but the trees were so thick and the ground so dark, I was afraid to leave the sight of our apartment complex. One Saturday when I walked to the edge of a clearing covered with tall grasses, I could see the sisters through the grass, sitting a short distance from me. I studied the group for a moment, wondering what life was like for them, but the sound of a fleeing bird distracted me and I looked away. Suddenly, I was startled by the sound of someone approaching and turned to find one of the sisters standing near me. Her rosy cheeks and broad smile relaxed me. She spoke to me warmly and was pleased that I could speak to her in German. She was happy to meet me and said I was welcome to join the sisters anytime I was in the forest. Her blue eyes sparkled through her wire-rimmed glasses. She reminded me of my grandmother, and I wanted to hug her, but I kept my seat and shook hands instead, saying, "Danke Schoen, Vielen Dank" (Thank you, thank you very much). When she rejoined the other sisters and spoke with them, she looked and pointed in my direction. They all smiled when I waved to them. They waved at me in return. I regret that

I did not join them, but I remembered my father's stern warning and stayed put.

On Sunday evenings when the weather was nice, my parents sat on the balcony, sipping a glass of wine and watching traffic on the heavily traveled road behind our apartment complex. Small German cars were bumper to bumper for hours as they drove back into the city after a day or weekend in the country. There were no street lights, and when the late-afternoon sun began to set and the sky turned from dusk to dark, the car headlights looked like a line of moving Christmas lights in the surrounding darkness. Quiet moments like these were special for my parents, and from the dining-room window I could see how much they enjoyed this time together.

Sometimes unexpected visitors, such as the flower lady who tried to sell Frank some flowers, came to the apartment complex. When unusual music floated up into the apartment through the back windows one day, we rushed to the balcony to find the source of the interesting sounds. Sitting in the grass behind our apartment building was a stout middle-aged German man dressed in traditional Bavarian clothing, playing a zither. He smiled and played hard, his arms plucking and stroking the zither, making beautiful music. Apartment residents threw coins in his hat nestled near his leg. He was a showman as well as a musician, and he was missing a leg. His crutch was well hidden in the grass, next to his good leg.

Sometimes on a Sunday Helga and Gerhard would take Frank and me swimming. On the way home, Gerhard would turn on the radio in his Mercedes Benz so frank could listen to *The Lone Ranger*. The Gruckenberg family often took us swimming in nearby Chiemsee during the summer. They always brought a picnic lunch with cold Loewenbrau, good Bavarian beer. We enjoyed being the only Americans in a group of German people. Frank and I found German children our age and had fun trying to understand each other using gestures. On Sunday afternoons in the fall, we often visited the Munich zoo and were startled to find the animals in their natural environments without cages or fences. Elephants were surrounded by a deep moat. They roamed their large plot as if they were in Africa or India.

"I don't want to go any closer," my mother said.

"Daddy, are those elephants really going to stay behind that water?" Frank asked.

"Yes," he answered. "They're not going any place."

"Look!" Frank shouted, pointing to the elephants. "That one has his toes in the water, and he's raising his trunk!" He also let out a loud squeal, but he stayed behind the moat.

We stood and watched for the longest time, making certain the elephants would not leave their secured area, but also because the animals were so beautiful in their natural setting. At Thanksgiving, my mother cooked for eight members of the Gruckenberg family on our tiny gas stove. There were twelve of us around the table exchanging Thanksgiving stories—their versions and ours. Both families tried testing the other for the meaning of words in their native language. It was a hilarious time, but with a delicious dinner.

I wondered what our German friends thought when they approached the large apartment complex in Perlacher Forst. Munich is the cultural center of Bavaria, but the drab, gray three-story apartment buildings all looked alike. In a sense it was a forest of large apartment buildings, each with black numerals painted on the front. We lived near the entrance of the complex. Our three-bedroom, one-bathroom apartment on the second floor of our building was not large, but we had adequate living space. Our bedroom closets were unusual in that we had large pullout drawers to place folded clothing. A rail over the drawers was for hanging shirts or pants. There was also a full closet for hanging dresses, suits, or uniforms in each bedroom. On the floor of the full closet was a rail to hold shoes in place. It was an efficient arrangement because we did not need much bedroom furniture. My mother had a gift for making every place we lived comfortable and attractive. All of our furniture was army issue. Washing machines and deep stainless steel sinks were in the basement of each apartment building. Clothesline trees were discreetly placed behind the apartment buildings. Clothesline ropes were strung across the length of the washroom by former residents.

This was all very different from our experience in Japan, where we had lived in an old Japanese house in downtown and were neighbors with Mama-san and Mr. and Mrs. Kimoto. We had lived in the Japanese culture, but we had been isolated because no one spoke English and we did not speak Japanese. When we moved to Mount Kurokuriyama, Hatsie had still come to work for us. But seven years after the war, except for Mama-san and Hatsie, who were so loving, cautious fear seemed to separate each culture. In Munich we lived in an American community. Nearby there were some small German restaurants, houses, and apartment buildings. We were close to the large Kasern, the base where my father worked, but we had to ride the bus or take a car into Munich to experience the German culture. The Gruckenberg family lived across Munich, an hour away. Although we met many German people, we did not have an opportunity to be close to someone like Mama-san. Language and location were the only things separating us from the German people, but we felt isolated in the large American community.

At Christmas Frank and I helped my mother decorate a real Christmas tree that we placed in front of the living-room window. My mother bought beautiful decorations in the Christkindlmarkt in nearby Augsburg. The German stores had crèches in the display windows and some displayed children's toys, but there were no lights or any commercial decorations like those we had known in the States. Homes were decorated with only a single candle in the window. We were fascinated by the simple beauty of German Christmas decorations in their homes as well as in their stores. Brightly colored lights in the windows of Perlacher Forst and Christmas trees decorated with colored lights and shiny decorations in living-room windows were fascinating to the German people who came in large groups to see the American decorations. We were invited to the Gruckenberg home to see their small tree with very long needles sitting on a table with a white candle on the end of each branch. There were no other decorations in the house. We sang "Stillige Nacht, Heilige Nacht" ("Silent Night, Holy Night"), and then Helga blew out the candles. Mrs. Gruckenberg served Lebkuchen, delicious sweet cookies she made. In spite of all this, we missed being at home during the holidays very much, and no one missed it more than my mother.

Military life had an important social aspect that required my parents' attendance. This occurred whenever there was a change in command, but there were also private parties given by friends. When they went out, my father wore his dress blues, and my mother wore a semiformal evening dress she had made. At home Frank and I listened to *Gunsmoke* on the radio while I made Kraft macaroni and cheese dinners for our supper. Sometimes I cut up pieces of ham and added a can of green peas to make a balanced meal. For dessert we ate large bowls of vanilla ice cream. Sometimes my parents played bridge with other couples in our apartment house, and they often invited people in for dinner.

For me, entertainment meant babysitting opportunities on Friday and Saturday nights for people in our apartment building. Sometimes, but not very often, I was allowed to spend the night with a school friend who lived in nearby Perlacher Forst apartments. Frank played kickball in the open area behind the apartments with other children who lived nearby. We both had so much homework there was time for little else.

After we had lived in Munich for about two years, many of the people we knew and liked were transferred back to the States. Large groups of new personnel and their families were transferred to Munich. We felt like 'the new kid on the block' again. We didn't know anybody and had to meet and make friends all over again. About this time my father prepared to go on maneuvers with his company for a week. When he had participated in previous maneuvers, he had only been away for a long weekend. I watched my father hug and kiss my mother good-bye at the front door. Their eyes were locked in a stare as they stood silently for a while. Then he opened the door and left quietly. He was wearing green army fatigues and combat boots, a holstered gun, and he carried a helmet with him. I had never seen him wearing fatigues or combat boots, or carrying a gun of any kind. My mother turned to me with a long face and said that he was going with his company to practice evacuating in case the Communists moved across the border of Czechoslovakia.

She looked so disheartened and said, "We'll never get out if they cross the border. There is no way they can get every American dependent and all military personnel out of Munich if the Communists move across the border." When I asked her where my father's company would be going, she said he didn't tell her.

Every military family was required to keep a box with three days' worth of canned food, candles, and matches. We had to be ready to leave on a moment's notice. I never realized the fear my mother must have felt when we lived in Munich. If my father felt fearful, he never showed it. On an October morning in 1957, after breakfast, Frank and I were getting ready to walk to school, when the radio announcer interrupted his program to report that the Russians had just shot a rocket called *Sputnik* into space. "I wonder what they're going to do next," my mother said. It was cause for concern. Our country was behind in space exploration. *Did that mean that we were behind militarily too?*

Berchtesgaden

My mother watched me as I boarded a large coach in front of Munich American High School. The ten-day Red Cross Leadership Camp in Berchtesgaden occurred the summer after my freshman year at Munich American High. I was active in the Junior Red Cross and I was thrilled when my parents allowed me to attend the camp. I didn't know what I was getting into, but I was anxious to go and learn. Several of my friends were going, and four of us planned to stay in the same room. I was looking forward to the opportunity to be an adult, but I was also frightened. I didn't really know any of these friends very well. I just spoke to them in the hallway or in class. In Houston, I was close to my cousins, but I wondered what it would be like to stay with people I didn't really know.

The bus ride from Munich to Chiemsee and then to Berchtesgaden took several hours. As we drove up into the mountains, we were mesmerized by beautiful Bavarian landscapes, rock-filled streams, and snow-covered mountaintops. In the afternoon we arrived at a mountain chalet. I was amazed at the surrounding beauty, the politeness of the staff, and the quality of our room. The first evening after dinner we watched a group of Bavarian folk dancers perform. I was fascinated by the traditional Bavarian clothing as well as the unusual dancing. Young women wore traditional dirndls, and young men wore lederhosen (leather shorts with wide suspenders to hold them up) and long-sleeved sweaters. They all wore thick, clunky shoes for dancing. As the band played, they twirled, hopped, and skipped in patterns to the music. Periodically, the men stopped and slapped the back of their pants, creating a loud popping noise. Other times they slapped the bottom of their heels loudly.

The next day we were in leadership meetings all day, but the following day there was a bus trip to see Hitler's Eagle's Nest. We boarded a heavy-duty, specially-built Mercedes-Benz coach and headed straight up the mountainside. As we followed the narrow, two-lane road up the mountain, the driver kept changing the gears to accommodate hairpin curves. I held onto my seat and held my breath, afraid to look out of the window into the deep chasm of dark-green trees and valleys. The bus ground its way slowly up the mountain to a flat surface. After a few minutes, steel doors hidden in the mountain walls opened, and the bus moved slowly into a large elevator. I was terrified and wondered where the driver was taking us. In another few minutes, the elevator started moving upward very slowly. The steel doors opened, and we drove out of the elevator onto a clearing and into the clouds.

A small wooden cottage rested on the edge of the mountaintop. There was little room to park. I was still frightened. I didn't know this was our destination and I was afraid we would drive over the edge, but the driver skillfully maneuvered the large coach until it was within the designated parking lines. We got off and walked through the mist of surrounding clouds and stood silently, absorbing the magnificent beauty. A bird call echoed through the snow-covered peaks. Sun rays broke through the clouds, enough to highlight the mountains surrounding us. It was colder than we expected, and we began to move toward the little cottage that had been the Eagle's Nest, now a tea room. Inside, the cottage looked like a Bavarian home in a small village. White curtains framed the windows, narcissus bloomed in pots, and a fire glowed in the large fireplace. Red-and-white-checked tablecloths covered dark wooden tables. We took a seat at one of the small, round tables, and a lovely young blonde waitress came to take our orders, hot tea with a piece of strudel. We sat in silence, gazing in wonder at this place that had so often been in the headlines.

It was easy to see why Hitler liked this place. I could see him meeting with Goering, Speer, and Himmler at a long table; drinking hot tea with whiskey or beer; eating schnitzel and strudel; orchestrating rallies; and drawing up plans to invade Poland, Belgium, Czechoslovakia, and France, feed the war machine, and build the death camps. Looking around in the small one-room cottage, I could almost feel the euphoria one gets when success feeds success. I could see him here with Eva Braun. I could understand how the two of them would love to come here just to get away from it all. But I did not understand how Hitler could be absorbed in the beauty of the mountains; breathe the pure, clean air; and watch an eagle soar from the mountaintops while he planned to annihilate people. My friends and I sat in silence, sipping our hot tea. While looking through the windows and taking in the beauty of the mountain peaks through the clouds, we wondered what else had occurred here.

Another day trip took us to Salzburg. The heavy-duty coach headed east over beautiful mountainous terrain with tiny villages tucked in the valleys below. Snow on the mountain peaks looked like white frosting running down the mountain. Clouds engulfed the highest peaks, giving them a mystical feeling. It was a fitting beginning for an unforgettable day. First, we toured Mozart's small childhood home. We saw the harpsichord he used to play sitting in his living room in front of the window facing the street.

We toured the Bishop's Palace next, which surprisingly was inhabited. A fascinating tour of the salt mines was next. (Is that why the city is named Salzburg?) Everyone lined up before a steep wooden shaft that headed down into the mines. We were handed a piece of leather to sit on. With only a few light bulbs hanging from the ceiling, it was hard to see. One by one, we slid down the deepest slide any of us had ever seen. It was a good thing we had a piece of leather to sit on, as our seats were red hot when we jumped up and tried to walk on the uneven rock surface of the mine. It was really cold, and I appreciated salt more after I experienced the necessary labor to extract a mineral that made our food so tasty. In a few minutes, we approached another wooden slide, were handed another piece of leather to sit on, and slid deeper into the mine. We walked for miles, it seemed, to see how the miners hacked away at the walls of the mountain with picks, loaded the extracted rocks into small metal cars, and hauled them out of the mine by hand. I couldn't wait to get back to the surface and away from the cold, damp, darkness we felt deep in the mine.

After we left the salt mines, we were driven to the catacombs near Salzburg, where early Christians hid to avoid persecution. Although history tells us about the persecutions of Christians in ancient Rome, they were not excluded from attacks and brutality elsewhere in Europe. Some were buried there in the mountainside cave we visited. After we entered the cool, dark cave, I had to stoop often to keep from hitting my head. In other places I had to turn sideways to fit through narrow passageways. We began to feel chilled, but kept walking, wondering why we were touring the long, narrow cave, when we came to a small coffin carved into the wall. A simple white candle in a small brass holder resting on the stone grave flickered bits of light onto the dark walls. I lingered for a moment. Staring at the unknown person buried in the mountain wall, I wondered what he or she had endured that I might walk freely into any house of worship, kneel, and pray. As I stood and stared at the coffin, I felt the presence of God within me. I was the last one to leave the cave, and when I did, I knew that the presence of God would always be with me. From that time on I became more curious about religion.

The return trip to Berchtesgaden was very quiet. For the rest of the conference we attended leadership meetings. In one session we were asked to name famous leaders and tell what characteristics they showed for leadership and how they became leaders. President Eisenhower and Winston Churchill were mentioned along with Napoleon, Adolf Hitler, and Benito Mussolini. Next we had to list what leadership characteristics we possessed and how we could best use them. Much discussion was created from this assignment. At the end of ten days, we boarded the heavy-duty coach and headed back to Munich. Being in Berchtesgaden for the Red Cross Leadership Conference prepared us for another year in Munich American High School as young adults, but it also prepared us for adulthood.

The Swimming Pool

One afternoon, Peggy, our neighbor who lived upstairs, took me to a swimming pool near the outskirts of Munich. She was a good friend of my mother's and a sponsor of my Girl Scout troop. Her husband worked in the German economy, was fluent in German, and knew interesting places in Munich that Americans did not. We drove for some time before she parked the car in front of a small wooden building, well hidden by birch trees. She let me out and said she would pick me up in about an hour because she had some shopping to do.

I walked into the building to discover that it was the women's dressing room. There were no privacy curtains and there were no showers, but all around the room there were wooden cubby-holes for storing one's clothes. I stood in front of an empty cubby-hole and began to undress with the German girls who had come in with me. No one spoke, but everyone was looking out of the corner of an eye to see if the American girl looked any different from the German girls without clothes on. The American girl was looking to see if the German girls were any different than she was without their clothes on. Both groups were well satisfied that without clothes, we all looked the same. I quickly pulled up my bathing suit and stuffed my jeans, cotton blouse, shoes, socks, and underwear into the cubby-hole in front of me.

I followed some of the girls through the open door into the pleasant pool area. The pool was hidden behind the birch trees, and there was a cyclone fence in front of the trees. It was not a large pool and did not have a diving board. A lot of people were in the water, and some people were sunning themselves in chairs on the concrete deck. I walked toward the middle of the pool and sat on the side for a moment to get my bearings. I studied the water and tried to estimate how deep it was and if there were a shallow end while my legs dangled over the edge. I couldn't come to any conclusion because there were so many people in the water. I decided to slip in and just hold on to the side for a while.

The cold water felt good and did not have the look or the smell of chlorine. Maybe it was spring water. I tried to stay out of the way when people swam near me. It wasn't long, though, before the area in front of me cleared, and I decided to swim across to the other side. It was then that I noticed a horrible burn scar across the back of a man near the end of the pool. His skin was so textured it appeared that the scar hadn't healed at all. It looked as if someone had taken a torch to the skin, melted it, and with his or her hands pushed it into a diagonal pile on his back. The scar seemed to pull away from the rest of the skin. It was red, ugly, and looked so painful. I turned away quickly just as a man with one leg pulled himself out of the pool. He sat on the side and let his good leg dangle in the water. The stump was horribly scarred. I was astonished. I had never seen such mutilation on human beings. Again I turned away, but a man with one arm was swimming in front of me. The stump of his missing arm flapped in the water, making noisy splashes. I could see terrible scarring on the end of his stump. I stared momentarily at these inequities even though I knew it was very rude. I headed to the side of the pool, got out of the water, and sat on the edge. What kind of place was this? Where did these people come from? How did they manage to live their daily lives?

I looked up at the trees to avoid looking at the men. How could this be? How could people swim without all their limbs? How could the man with a horribly scarred back expose himself to others? I looked down at the water, making every effort not to look at anyone. Was everyone in this pool scarred or maimed in some way? None of the girls in the dressing room were scarred or missing any limbs. No one else seemed to have noticed anything different about the men in the pool except me. Maybe I was the one who was different. I had not experienced physical tragedy, and I didn't know anyone who had.

I looked across the pool at the man with the scarred back. From the front, he was a very nice-looking man. In fact, he was a handsome, middle-aged man. I looked again at the man with one leg and the man with one arm. They too were very nice-looking men. They really didn't even look like they were middle-aged. Somehow, they seemed to have recognized my confusion. They knew, as did everyone else at the pool, that I had not experienced the tragedy of war and that I had never seen anyone with missing limbs or with horrible burn scars.

Once again, I looked across the pool and into the eyes of the men who had suffered. They nodded solemnly, and I looked down into the water. The top of my suit had almost dried, but my legs were still dangling in the water. I slipped in and started swimming up and down the length of the pool, trying not to bump into anyone. The water felt really good. I remembered how good it used to feel when I went swimming in the States. I looked up when I reached the end of the pool and saw people standing there on the concrete deck. They all had two legs. I looked up a little more and saw that they all had two arms as well. I turned around in the water and swam back to my spot near the middle of the pool.

The man with one arm was swimming in front of me, the stump of his missing arm making splashes whenever it hit the water. The man with one leg was swimming too. They swam better than I did. The man with the burn scar was a great swimmer. I wished that I could swim as well as all of these men. What would life have been like for them if they had not experienced the horror of war? What chance at a normal life did they have now? I was stunned by the sight of their missing limbs and scarred stumps, their awkward movements. I didn't want to be in the water with them. But I couldn't justify my feelings. I couldn't look the men in the face or look at their wounds any longer. Is this what war is really about? What protected my father from those same wounds? It was then I realized that in many ways I lived a comfortably sheltered life. I sat on the side of the pool again and wondered how different my life would be if someone in our family suffered the way these men had. I wouldn't treat that person any differently, and I would give as much support as I could. Then I realized that accepting physical differences in people who did not look or walk as I did was not so difficult.

An Old Woman

Snowdrifts covered the sides of the roads, but as we drove north on the Autobahn (highway), we took in the beauty of a winter wonderland. It was midwinter and very cold, but my parents loved to drive through Bavaria on weekends, taking in the sights and sounds of local culture and the beauty of the mountains. We had been living in the rich cultural center of Bavaria for eighteen months, and now we all missed being in the States, especially during holidays. My parents missed their families as much as Frank and I did.

We drove to Nurnberg, where the war trials were held, on a Sunday. As we approached the outskirts of the town, we came to the enormous stadium where Hitler held his huge rallies. My father slowed the car to a stop. "God Damn, ... would you look at that," he said under his breath. We sat in silence for a while and just stared at the enormity of it, the history of it. I thought about the newsreels of the Nazi rallies held at this stadium: thousands of young people, most of them waving flags, everyone happy and smiling, shouting, "Heil Hitler! Heil Hitler!" Nazi soldiers marched in formation on the stadium grounds, and Adolf Hitler screamed from the podium. As we sat there, I wondered what was going through my father's mind. We were in one of the hotbeds of Nazism. Was he thinking of the D-day invasion? The furious fighting and the bombings as Germans and Americans tried to annihilate each other only thirteen years ago? The human cost of war? The quiet empty stadium resonated with Nazi ghosts screaming, "Heil Hitler! Heil Hitler!"

We drove on in stunned silence. We reached the city, which looked as if all of it had been bombed to pieces and then rebuilt. New pink stone replaced missing parts in the old city wall. Most of the buildings had been rebuilt with the same pink stone, giving the city a strange two-toned look. We examined every building and home we passed closely for signs of war damage. Maybe some of them had been significant to the Nazi war effort. *Who inhabited that building before the war, during the war? Was anyone living there now?* We looked at every passing face as my father drove slowly through very narrow streets, which had room for only one car. *Was that person a former Nazi? Did those people attend rallies at the stadium?* I hoped that no one would attack our car the way we were attacked in Hiroshima.

Pedestrians walked hurriedly along, ignoring us, acting as if we were not even driving on the city streets. They must have had a specific purpose for being outside in the bitter cold, moving in pairs or in small groups as quickly as possible, dressed in heavy dark coats, boots, hats, scarves, and gloves. As we passed by one group and then another, no one smiled or spoke. Ours was the only car on the streets that morning. *Was everyone else in church?*

My father drove slowly over snow-covered brick streets, headed for the center of the city, and turned a narrow corner. An old fountain was sticking out of the snow, and water frozen in beautiful shapes cascaded down the sides; behind it stood an old building, painted a soft yellow. My father paused for us to look when my mother said, "Look at that old woman walking in the snow. She looks so pitiful. Stop the car, honey. Roll down the window. Mary Lou, say something to her."

My father stopped the car as the old woman approached our blue Ford sedan without noticing us. Frank wound down his window.

"Ask her if she needs a ride, Mary Lou," my mother said.

"Entschuligen Sie Mir, bitte. Durfen sie mit uns in dem auto nehmen, bitte?" (Excuse me, may we please give you a ride in the car with us?)

"Was?" (What?), the old woman replied with indignation.

"Durfen sie mit uns in dem auto nehmen, bitte?" I repeated.

A short black scarf covered her silver hair. Dull, blue eyes and deep wrinkles composed her tired, thin face. She looked into the car with a frown and then looked at each of us sternly.

"Bitte?" (Please?), I asked again. She looked at me and smiled a little, nodded to my parents.

"Move over by me," I whispered to Frank. He moved over and looked at the old woman again. The car was cold inside now, but none of us moved or spoke. She eyed the inside of the car hungrily. We sat quietly staring, waiting for her decision.

"Ja," she said suddenly, nodding her head. She climbed into the back seat with a smile, happy to be out of the cold, damp snow. She sat still, expecting my father to move the car forward, but she didn't know the door had to be closed first and made no effort to close it. Frank and I kept looking at the open door. My parents also waited for her to close the door. It was very cold in the car now, and the old woman was no longer smiling.

"She doesn't know how to close the door," I said finally. My father strained, reached way back and grasped the door by the silver handle, pulling it firmly forward until it closed. Observing my father's every move, the old woman leaned away from the door and close to Frank. She was frightened, but did not want to get back out in the cold and snow. My parents smiled at her and turned around. My father accelerated forward slowly while he turned the heat up high.

"Ask her where she's going," my mother said to me.

"Wo gehen sie, bitte?" (Where are you going, please?)

"Dortdruben" she said. "Nach die Bahnhoff fur den jungen zu sehen." She gave a wide smile and pointed straight ahead.

"She's going to the train station to see her son," I said.

"Oh, hell, where's the damn train station?" my father mumbled.

"I think she said it was over there," I answered, pointing straight ahead just as the woman had done. We drove very slowly for about eight blocks. We passed several groups of people to whom she waved and smiled warmly. Her friends looked at her in shock and stopped walking to stare at the slowly passing blue Ford while the old woman chuckled to herself. We kept driving slowly forward. The train station was nowhere in sight. Suddenly, she said, "Danke schoen" (Thank you), and with her left hand pulled up the door handle. The door unlocked and began to open. "She opened the door!" I said, alarmed. My father quickly stepped on the brakes, and we all rocked forward. She jumped out and stood with the door open, smiling warmly and gratefully. My father was caught off guard and waited for her to close the door again, but she didn't touch it or even reach for it. My mother was saddened by her sudden departure.

"Close the door, Frank," my father said firmly but quietly. Frank reached over, smiling at the old woman and said good-bye while reaching for the door handle. "Auf Wiedersehen" (Good-bye), we said, waving to her as Frank shut the door. She waved slightly and continued to smile. Her blue eyes sparkled, and her wrinkles had faded. My father accelerated forward very slowly again. Frank and I turned around and looked out of the back window. She was standing still, waving, smiling broadly. Frank and I kept waving too, expecting her to continue walking again, but she didn't move at all. She stood motionless in the same place, her black coat a stark contrast to the brilliant white snow as she grew smaller and smaller in the distance.

A Trip to Paris

We had breakfast in our hotel and walked a half block to the Champs Elysees. The wide boulevard was filled with moving traffic. Striped awnings covered tables and chairs in the sidewalk cafés where well-dressed people sat drinking coffee and reading the morning paper. We walked slowly for a few blocks and then came to a hotel with a brass front and a large revolving door. My father turned abruptly and passed through the door. Through the glass wall in the lobby, he smiled and signaled that we should follow him. As we entered, the uniformed bell hop approached and in broken English asked for our luggage. My father made excuses and then went to use a lobby telephone. Frank stood close to my mother. I wondered what my father was doing and why we were in this hotel lobby, watching elegantly dressed people passing in and out of the revolving glass doors. I had never seen such beautiful women or women so beautifully groomed. In a few minutes my father was back with a big smile on his face.

"She's there," he said. "She said to come up. Let's go."

I didn't know my father knew anyone in France, much less in Paris. From the look on my mother's face, I don't think she did either. He walked hurriedly into the crowds on the street.

"Where are we going?" Frank asked.

"To see somebody," my father answered quickly. "You people need to move faster," he added, "and watch where you are going."

Walking with Parisians on this famous boulevard, we did our best to keep up with him while taking in the sights and sounds and smells of a magical city. After walking nearly five blocks, my father stopped in front of a grand, old building. Smiling, he took a piece of paper from his pocket and glanced at the writing, and then he pushed a brass button near the door. A woman's voice came over the intercom.

"Oui?"

"Louise, it's Carl," my father replied anxiously.

"Oui, Carl! Come!" the voice gushed with excitement and a heavy French accent.

"Okay!" he laughed.

"Who is she?" Frank asked my mother. "Do we know this lady?"

"No," my mother said quietly.

"Why are we coming here?" he asked.

"Daddy wants to see his old friend," my mother said, making this easier for Frank to understand.

With the sound of the buzzer, the large wooden door opened. We entered a marble vestibule and passed eight brass mailboxes in the left wall on our way to the elevator. My father was smiling from ear to ear. Frank stood close to my mother, who looked frightened. My heart was pounding. I did not know what to expect or who we would meet in the apartment. My father pushed the brass button, and when the elevator door opened we stepped into an ornate, but faded interior. With the push of a shiny button numbered six, the old door closed and we started moving up leisurely. On the sixth floor, it stopped; the door creaked and opened slowly. We stepped out onto the marble floor and followed my father down the hall to apartment number 628. He was beaming as he rang the doorbell, still holding the small piece of paper in both hands.

It was a long time before the door opened, but when it did, there stood a short, well-dressed woman with an abundance of curly gray and black hair. She fell into my father's arms as she said, "Carl." They embraced warmly before she broke away to welcome us into her home. She shook hands with each of us as my father made introductions.

This charming, plump woman was middle-aged and could hardly speak English, but she never stopped smiling or talking. As she showed us through her living room and dining room, we could see a panorama of the city skyline through the large windows. The apartment was impeccably clean and tastefully decorated. We followed her into the small white kitchen and stood around the worktable in the middle of the room. She talked nonstop to my father while waving her arms up and down, back and forth. I did not understand anything she was saying, and neither did my parents.

My father seemed very comfortable with the woman, but we were not invited to sit down. She did not take any cups and saucers out of the cabinets or offer tea and coffee. If she had, we might have stayed for a while. She kept moving from the stove to the small sink and back to the work table in the center of the kitchen. She mentioned to my father that her husband was working and would be home for lunch soon, but she could not take her eyes off of my father.

We edged our way back through the elegant apartment toward the front door while the woman followed behind us, talking nonstop. She seemed relieved that we were not going to stay. My father was disappointed she did not offer an invitation to stay longer. We shook hands again. My father embraced the woman once again very warmly and kissed her good-bye on the left cheek. She responded with a warm hug and kissed my father on both cheeks before releasing her embrace. As we passed through the front door, she stood staring at my mother, Frank, and me with large black eyes. Just before she closed the door, her hand waved good-bye.

We walked back to the elevator. My father pushed the button, and the creaking door opened. We filed in silently, the door closed, and we began our descent. There was a slight bump as the elevator touched the ground floor. We exited and walked toward the old front door, our footsteps echoing throughout the vestibule. We passed the brass mailboxes and through the wooden door. My father tried to hide the sadness and disappointment on his face as he quietly shut the door.

He had been in Paris during the war, although he never mentioned it before our visit. What transpired during that time when he first knew the woman? Did he stay here with her family? Was she in love with my father then? Was he in love with her? Why didn't she invite us to stay and meet her husband?

We retraced our steps down the Champs Elysees toward our hotel, looking for an appropriate place to eat lunch, and stopped at a small bistro near the hotel. As we ate soup, a salad, and French bread, my father talked about other places in Paris he wanted us to see. Meeting Louise and seeing her apartment took my mother by surprise, but she kept her feelings to herself. I wondered about my father and the war. Frank ate his lunch quietly. My mother did not speak during lunch until he said he wanted to take us to the Eiffel Tower. She wanted to go up to the top. She mentioned something about taking a tour of the city, but my father was not the type to tour with a group. He was an explorer and wanted to discover places on his own.

After we finished our lunch we returned to the hotel, and got into the car. I kept thinking about Louise. Is that why we really came here? My father drove on the Champs Elysees passing the opera house, along the Seine River, and past Notre Dame before parking near the Eiffel Tower. We stood in line and paid for our tickets before entering the small elevator packed with people. It was really a four-sided cage in the middle of the tower, and it began to swing every which way as soon as it started moving up. We stood at the perimeter of the cage and held on to the metal rail as we moved slowly upward. Without warning, it stopped in the middle of the tower. The operator said if we wanted to go to the top we would have to pay a few more francs. My father hesitated, but my mother wanted to see the city from the top. The sun was beginning to set and cast gorgeous arrays of light on the Seine and the city skyline. My father handed over the extra francs as did the few people left in the cage. The operator closed the door, and we began our ascent to the top.

Eight people crowded onto the small platform and stood facing west, watching the sun sink as the last rays painted the City of Light every color of the rainbow. How could anyone forget this? It was so beautiful that no one spoke and no one moved.

A cool breeze blew through the tower. Cars below driving with their headlights on created a parade of moving lights. I wondered if my father had been here on the Eiffel Tower thirteen years earlier, and what he saw when the city was liberated from the Germans.

While I was writing this book, I reread my father's WWII diary. I found the following names and addresses, along with many other names and addresses, in the front. He never spoke about Louise, and we never learned how he knew her, but in one diary entry he writes that he was sent to school in Paris after D-day. Then he wrote that "one could live in Paris."

Madame Marcelle Boulanger
10 rue Git le Coeur
Paris 6 ieme

Raoult
9 rue Leon Vandoyer
Paris 7 ieme

An Education

The American school for dependents in Munich was very challenging. A student could make a 100 on every paper and every test and still get a grade of C, because that is what an average student would do. For an A or even a B, students were expected to do extra-credit reports or projects along with daily assignments. I earned a C in one of my classes when I had made a 90 to 100 on every paper and test. I was devastated. At home, I couldn't stop crying. This made me feel I was incapable of doing the required work, despite of all the hard work I had done. My parents could not console me, but my mother went to see the school counselor. During the next grading period my grades were again in the 90s, but I did some extra-credit work and brought my grade up to a B. My father, who was attending the University of Maryland in the evenings, helped me with math. One of our neighbors downstairs, who was fluent in German, helped me with my German homework. Still I was up until midnight or later every night trying to finish all my homework, and I never completed all of it. At school we formed groups and shared homework results, which helped a lot. I was good in history and English so I shared my homework with others in our group of four or five who were good in math and science. It was 1958; Frank was in fifth grade, and I was a sophomore.

Despite the amount of homework assignments I had, I volunteered to work in the library during my free period every day. I helped the head librarian check in new books and helped students check out books. I loved having access to books when no one else did. I played volleyball well and was on the school team. We traveled by bus to American high schools in other German cities for competitions. It was one of the activities I enjoyed most. I sang in the choir and performed with choir members for school events. Once we were invited to sing in a restaurant during the lunch hour in downtown Munich. The restaurant was packed with German people who greatly appreciated our performance.

Later that year, Ms. Gardner, our choir teacher, took six students who were interested in opera to see Aiida in the National Theater. We rode the bus from Munich High School, then took a city bus to the theater on a school night. With student tickets, we sat in the back of the beautiful theater. The costumes, the music, and real white horses on the stage at the end of the opera, convinced me that I wanted to be an opera singer. One of the largest school choir performances took place in the Nurnberg Opera House, and I was very fortunate to be part of the choir from Munich. American high school choirs from France and southern Germany performed *Die Meistersinger von Nurnberg* as a gift to the German people. We practiced singing all year, and our performance was well received. It was a proud moment I will never forget.

Herr Schmalzbauer, who taught first-year German, was a no-nonsense teacher with a good disposition, who made learning fun. I'd heard rumors of Frau Hellerer's teaching style from former students: humiliating students for no apparent reason, sudden bursts of outrage, screaming tirades uttered beneath a coy smile. Now that I was in a second-year German class, I would find out exactly what Frau Hellerer's teaching style was really like.

I entered the room where second-year German was taught, looking for a seat far enough away from the teacher's desk to hide my face if the need arose, yet close enough to copy every word from the board without straining. On every desk there was a book. She was sitting at her desk writing and did not acknowledge anyone's presence as students filed in looking for a seat.

As soon as the bell rang, Frau Hellerer jumped up from her desk and closed the door. "Open your books to page one," she said. She covered the material on the page quickly and moved to conversations on page two, speaking in rapid *Hochdeutsch* (high German), and writing on the board in script to emphasize certain points in the book. No one moved. Because she moved through the material so quickly, it was difficult at times to understand her or to read her writing. Then she called on someone to read a short paragraph in the textbook. She gave advice to the student for improving his reading technique. She asked questions about the material to check for understanding and expected immediate responses without errors.

Her short, round body danced back and forth in front of the blackboard, while her hand periodically made perfect letters of script into meaningful words. Her dark-blonde hair was always pulled tightly into a bun at the back of her head. Brilliant blue eyes bore into the faces of students as she assessed the class. She wore heavy black-soled shoes with laces and thick, flesh-colored stockings. Her loose-fitting skirt and tailored blouse complemented her body shape. She wore a few tasteful pieces of jewelry.

At the start, she gave her expectations for excellence, then assigned homework and continued to talk until the bell rang and students silently filed into the hall.

My fear of Frau Hellerer was justified the following day when she berated a student who raised his hand to ask a question while she was still talking. "Don't interrupt the teacher!" she screamed. "What is the matter with you? How will you learn if you keep interrupting the teacher? Pay attention! You students are all alike! You think you know everything! You know nothing! Nothing at all! When you pay attention, you don't need to ask so many questions!" Her hands conducted a symphony of anger during this outburst.

Every person in the class was expected to participate by answering her questions and reading out loud. There were students who had a background in German because either one or both parents were German. Other students had lived in Germany for some time and had experience with the language. I struggled to keep up with the assignments, making only Cs.

Mostly I struggled to hide my fear of her and my fear of being called on to speak German in class.

However, after class had been in session for about eight weeks, I raised my hand, shyly. With an encouraging smile, she said, "Mary Lou." I read the paragraph with a halting, creaky voice while sweat poured off me. She sat down at her desk when I was about halfway through the short story. When I finished, she smiled once again and said, "Very good." But she knew, as I knew, and the class knew that it was not good at all.

I never knew why she was so nice to me. I had been shaking all over, trying so hard not to make a mistake. Perhaps she gave me credit for that, but I was so relieved that she didn't scream at me.

Her distaste for anything American was often apparent, and her angry outbursts occurred regularly. "You should go to the museums while you are here," she told us. "The Deutsches Museum is known throughout the world. When you get back to the United States, people will ask you what you saw in Muenchen. What will you say except that you went to the basketball game or the football game or the movie and show once again that you know nothing of Germany, nothing at all?" she sneered.

Throughout the fall, I learned much of the history of Prussia and Germany. "Germany is great in every area," she told us. "No other country has been so famous in art, history, music, politics, and science. No one can change that and no one can take it away from us!" she would shout. "Even the United States would not be what it is today if the Hessians had not come to rescue the Americans during the Revolutionary War. Yes, it was George Washington who begged them to come and fight because he knew they were the best!"

Astonished at this historical viewpoint, I began to share this information with my parents and Frank at the supper table, but my father exploded at the idea of Germany helping the United States prevail during the American Revolution. I could almost see steam coming out of his ears as he negated each of Frau Hellerer's statements. "I know how good the goddamn Germans are," he roared. "I was in the invasion! On the beaches of France during the D-day invasion! I know!" he shouted glaring at me, leaning over toward me. "I know! I was there!" Fire was coming out of his eyes. I thought he was going to lunge across the table at me. I was terrified and didn't understand his response at all. Was this the same man I knew as my father? Didn't he want to be friends with Mr. and Mrs. Gruckenberg and their family members? Didn't we have them come to our apartment? Didn't he drive us on weekends to areas around Munich to see the natural beauty of Bavaria? Didn't he point out the farmers and how hard they worked, the beautiful hand-painted pictures on the buildings in the villages? Didn't he enjoy eating Wiener schnitzel?

I was speechless and nearly breathless; so was my mother. Gently, Frank asked my father if he'd received a Purple Heart at the end of the war. My father's face became extremely red. After a brief silence he uttered a humble, "No," under his breath. There was a thick, uncomfortable silence around the table. Suddenly my mother said quietly, "Uncle Edward did." Uncle Edward was my mother's youngest brother and godfather to both Frank and me. My father finished his meal in complete silence, his eyes glued to his plate. His face remained very red. He never talked about his experiences in the war to us, although Frank often questioned him about it. We only heard him talk about his WWII experience when we visited the Gruckenberg family. I did not expect this response, and it was not my intention to cause such an angry outburst. When Frank opened his mouth to ask another question, my father jumped up from the table and grabbed him by the arm. "Get up!" he shouted, taking off his belt and heading for Frank's bedroom, next to our dining room, pushing Frank in front of him. "NO! DADDY, NO!" he shouted, struggling to pull away. "No!" he whimpered. My father shoved him through the doorway to the hall and into his bedroom while Frank tried his best to resist and escape. What had I done? I had only related what I learned in school. I watched in horror as my brother disappeared through the door screaming, "NO!"

I sat at the table, frozen to my chair as the belt pounded my brother. I felt the whelps all over my body. My mother abruptly jumped up from the table, looking horrorstricken, and went into the kitchen. I couldn't listen to my brother's screaming any more. I didn't know what to do. I was in shock. I wanted to save my brother, but I remained terrified of my father's power. I picked up my plate and went into the kitchen to see my mother quietly weeping and eating at the same time. "Beat him half to death ..." she mumbled, swallowing food and trying to suppress her tears. I was paralyzed. I needed to help my mother, but didn't know how, so I went back to the table and removed the plates and silverware. I went back into the kitchen and started scraping and washing the dishes. Finally, the belt stopped, and my brother's screams quieted. We withdrew into our own silent worlds for the rest of the evening. I never made any more comments about my German studies.

This event caused a schism in my parents' relationship, and from that time on my mother argued with my father about everything. My father seemed to be angry or sad all the time. He was remorseful about his treatment of Frank, but it was too late. Family dynamics were permanently altered.

My father felt that in her eyes his war experience did not equal that of her younger brother. After his death, my brother and I found his top dresser drawer full of medals and ribbons. A Purple Heart is awarded for injury in battle, but there was not one among my father's medals.

All of my uncles and cousins in my parents' generation, on both sides of the family, joined the military and were sent overseas during WWII, but Uncle Edward had been wounded in France. He was cowered down in a fox hole while American troops were advancing on the Germans. An American tank attempted to drive over the hedgerow where Uncle Edward lay on the other side in the foxhole. Fortunately, the tank could not make it up the hedgerow, had to back up, and make a jump over it, just missing Uncle Edward by a few feet. It then seemed very quiet and he raised his head to look around just as a bomb burst. Shrapnel hit the left side of his head. When he called for medics, they came with a stretcher, and rushed him to a helicopter. He wanted to take his helmet with him, but the medics did not want to delay getting him to the helicopter. He was transported to a hospital in London. A metal plate was placed over the shrapnel lodged in his head. While there, General Patton came to see him. When he recovered enough, he was transferred to McCloskey

Hospital in Temple, Texas where he stayed for nine months. He was told that he would never be able to work, drive, swim, or perform other tasks, however, he did all of those things. He was honorably discharged from the Army at nineteen after twelve months of service and awarded a Purple Heart. My father never talked about his experiences in WWII. We did not know that he had been in Korea until after his death. Is this why he often seemed to be in another place, removed from the present? Is this why he was so edgy, so sensitive to sounds?

The school year concluded at the end of May. I learned enough German to pass with a B, and my verbal skills had jumped significantly. We had read poems by Schiller and short stories by Goethe. After Frau Hellerer spoke eloquently about Thomas Mann, I went to the library in McGraw Kasern, where my father worked and checked out an English version of a book by him; it was the shortest one of his books on the shelf. My parents depended on me to translate when we were traveling. The language I heard on the street, Plattdeutsch (low German) spoken in Bavaria, was not what I learned in class, Hochdeutsch (high German). When I spoke German I was understood, but often I had to ask, "Sagen sie es mir noch einmal, bitte" (Can you repeat that to me, please?) so I could understand what was said to me. My rosy cheeks, which I inherited from my father, often invited unexpected conversation.

During the summer we spent weekends exploring the area around us, taking in the rich beauty of Bavaria. One Sunday my father took us on a special outing. Dressed in Sunday clothes, we got in our blue Ford and headed for Dachau. Although the camp was not active, I had been there a number of times because my friend Barbara and her family lived in one of the two-story red brick houses built for the officers at Dachau, but I had never been to the prison camp. I had a number of friends at Munich High whose families lived in those large two-story red brick houses in Dachau.

When I spent the night with Barbara, whom I'd met on the ship heading to Germany, we often walked to the barbed-wire fences and looked into the field on the other side. Tall grasses and wildflowers covered the ground. Small, windowless buildings, faded red, dotted the desolate field. Sometimes we could hear a door hinge creaking as the wind, sweeping the air clean, banged a loose door against a dilapidated building. Another time we went to the camp with a group of friends to explore what we could with our eyes. We dared each other to climb through the barbed wire and scout around, but no one had enough nerve to even touch the wire.

Barbara's family maid told them people in town knew something was wrong there, because people went in, but they never came out. Townspeople sneaked out to the camp and gave food to the prisoners, even though it was very dangerous to do that.

My family passed the sign in front, *Arbeit Macht Frei* (Work Makes You Free) and arrived at the official gate entrance; there were crowds of German people entering. They had come by the busloads, in cars, on bicycles, and on foot. We were the only Americans present. The sun was shining brightly; the air was crisp and cool. "They would bring them in here, line them up, and then shoot them," my father explained. "The concrete troughs in the ground were built to let the blood drain off." We were standing in a beautiful grassy rectangle, but listening to my father I was so stunned by the reality of the camp, I began to feel as if I had been shot myself. Frank stood close to my mother and held her hand tightly. She stood perfectly still, looking aghast at the concrete troughs.

We moved along to other areas of the camp and entered the showers. The room looked just like a dormitory shower room, but there were heavy steel doors with massive handles instead of shower curtains. I walked into one of them and touched the shower head. It was no different from the one in our bathroom. My mother told me to come out immediately, which I did. My father walked ahead of us, and we followed behind, wishing silently that we could just leave. In one building, lampshades had been crafted from human skin, and in another building, scientific experiments had been carried out. Finally, we reached the crematorium. I stood close and stared while my mother and Frank stood back. The brick ovens were so small, and rusted from use. They were connected to a large furnace that was directly behind them. I was numbed and horrified to think that human bodies had been dumped like trash into these ovens and burned. What kind of unconscionable animals had done this?

The last room was filled with pictures of emaciated people, some in baggy, striped clothing; others in remnants of clothing. There were pictures with piles of people stacked on top of each other, arms and legs sticking out in every direction. Mounds of bleached white bones were pictured behind barbed-wire fences. With skin stretched tightly over their bodies, holding their bones together, emaciated people stood together like puppets. Pictures of emaciated people hanging onto the barbed-wire fence for support were everywhere. Pictures with crowds of emaciated people, their mouths open, pressing into the fence, arms and legs reaching desperately for something, revealed some of the horrible cruelty in the camp. These photographs made me ask again, what kind of unconscionable animals had done this? None of the people in the pictures looked human at all.

We exited the camp and walked among quiet crowds of German people through the parking lot to our car. A gentle wind blew as if to clean the air, moving the flowers back and forth. Leaves shimmered in the trees. My mind was swimming with scenes from the camp. I couldn't connect the camp, what had occurred there, to the wonderful German people whom we knew and loved. How could this have happened? It was real, but it how could it have happened?

Like the trip to Hiroshima five years earlier, the trip to Dachau was unexpected. My father always wanted us to know "what it was like on the other side". We walked through Dachau, absorbing the appalling methods used to cripple and murder humans. In Hiroshima we sat in the car when a group of Japanese men attacked our car and tried to disable it, leaving us helpless.

Judy's father took this picture of me on the ferry as we crossed from Le Harve, France to Dover, England. The Cliffs of Dover are in the background.

A Camping Trip

When I was expected to have a project for the science fair in the spring of 1959, Sue Ellen's father, who was a veterinarian, helped me gather materials. I decided to do an experiment in a book I borrowed from the doctor who lived downstairs from us. A picture showed how blood was pumped through the heart. Sue Ellen's father read the description of the project and decided a cow's heart would be just the thing to demonstrate how the heart pumps blood. He found a nice one in the German market, and I brought it home from Sue Ellen's wrapped in newspaper on my bicycle. My mother allowed me to put it in the refrigerator for a few days because it was a science project, but it had to be out of the apartment before it started to smell. I borrowed two large syringes from the doctor who was our neighbor, and my father brought me a large square of plywood to secure everything. I proudly took my project to school and returned in the evening for the judging. Luckily, I didn't place high enough to go on to the district science fair, but I earned a B+ on my project, which boosted my science grade.

Sue Ellen's parents often invited me to go with her on weekend outings. We saw *Ben-Hur* in a wide-screen German theater when it was released. We also went to art galleries with her parents. On weekends we rode our bikes in Perlacher Forst, stopping in her house or mine for a snack or a drink before riding off again. Sue Ellen was a year older than me and was my best friend in

Munich High. I was thrilled when her parents invited me to go on a camping trip to London with them.

We drove across Germany into northern France in one day. When we stopped at the campground in France, Sue Ellen and I spotted a large swimming pool nearby. No one was in the pool or lounging around sunbathing. We couldn't wait to get in the water. We would have the entire pool to ourselves. Sue Ellen and I stuffed our long legs in the back-seat of her parents' Carmen Ghia, and her parents stuffed all the camping gear in the trunk.

While her parents set up the tent, we helped unload the rest of the gear. Then we unpacked our suits and changed quickly. It was already five o'clock. Her parents started the campfire and began to organize supper. We each grabbed a towel, wrapped it around our bodies, and proceeded to walk to the pool. As we came closer, we noticed the eight-foot-tall cyclone fence and the unlocked gate that surrounded the pool area. We marched through the gate and dropped our towels near the side of the pool. Bathing caps in place, we jumped into the cold water and started moving around to warm up.

We were walking into the deeper water when we heard a loud whistle blowing. Casually we turned to look in the direction of the sound and saw a French policeman outside the cyclone fence flapping his arms up and down like a bird as frantically as he was blowing the whistle. His black eyes were about to pop out of his head. Where did he come from? Why didn't he come inside the fence, walk to the pool, and address us directly? His behavior was confusing to us. We did not understand what we had done wrong, or why he was making a scene by constantly blowing his whistle.

The whistle attracted pedestrians from the neighborhood. A small crowd pressed into the fence, talking loudly. Heads turned from left to right and then stared straight ahead at the two American girls in the water.

"I think he's waving at us," I said. "I wonder what he wants."

"I don't know," Sue Ellen answered. "Look at all those people. I wonder what they want." The policeman continued blowing his silver whistle. His face turned red, and he moved his arms up and down fiercely.

"We haven't done anything wrong. We didn't see any 'No Swimming' signs, did we?" I asked.

"No," she said, "but I think we better get out before he comes to get us out with all those people following him."

"I think you're right," I said. "Let's get out before they come in. Your parents would be upset." We started retracing our steps to the shallow end where we'd jumped in. The policeman was not pleased at all when he saw us moving toward the opposite end of the pool. More pedestrians joined the loud group at the fence. It's not easy to walk in four feet of water, but we did the best we could. We decided to walk instead of swim so the policeman wouldn't misinterpret our actions.

He continued to blow the whistle; his arms kept moving wildly up and down. The crowd kept growing and getting louder. People started poking their fingers through the fence at the American girls in the water. Where did so many people come from? Were they just standing around looking for something to do? We did not understand any of this and couldn't wait to get back to the campground. We looked for any warning signs about the pool on the way but did not see any.

We reached the end of the pool and jumped out, grabbed our towels, and wrapped them around us as we moved through the open gate. We headed quickly toward our campsite, leaving the anxious policeman and the noisy crowd behind us. There was no explanation about the pool, and we did not want to be the target of angry French citizens, especially since we were foreigners. Sue Ellen's parents had supper waiting for us. We did not reveal our misadventure at the pool to them, but after supper, we decided to explore the campsite, which ran parallel to the highway.

We walked up the hill overlooking the campers and spotted a group of four handsome, young Frenchmen eating in front of their tent. We threw small pebbles at their plates. They ignored us and kept eating. We decided to throw small stones instead. They continued to ignore us. At this second affront, we stopped giggling and started throwing small rocks to appease our wounded feelings. We wanted to be noticed by the young Frenchmen, who were wearing berets, striped T-shirts, and jeans, but they were unmoved by our primitive efforts to get their attention.

Their plates were almost clean when, finally, the tallest one said in English, "Okay, you can stop now. We know you are up there. We can see you throwing stones." He put a french fry in his mouth, and the young man next to him said, "Yes, you can stop now. We can see you up there." We burst into excited giggles. We had their attention, but they didn't invite us to come down and join them. We dropped our handfuls of rocks, sneaked away from the campsite, and continued our walk on the side of the highway. Sue Ellen's parents warned us not to lose sight of the campground. We followed the two-lane highway to the opposite end of the campsite and sauntered back through the campers, hoping to encounter the handsome young Frenchmen. Like most of the other campers, they must have retired to their tent. Maybe in the morning, we agreed, maybe in the morning we'll see them. To our disappointment, there was no time to flirt with handsome Frenchmen after breakfast. Sue Ellen's parents had everything packed and in the car before we could really wake up, although we were expected to help. We had tickets for the ferry at Calais for ten o'clock that morning and reservations at the London campground for that evening, but we had to arrive before dark.

The Carmen Ghia was so small that the fee to cross was minimal. We drove onto the ferry without incident and got out to enjoy the ride across the English Channel. I wore a heavy woolen sweater my mother had bought in Germany, jeans, and a scarf, but I was still cold. Sue Ellen and her parents wore jackets, hats, and scarves. The stunning White Cliffs of Dover watched over the channel like ancient sentinels as the ferry moved us through the choppy waters. It took the rest of the day to drive from Dover to the London campsite. We arrived in plenty of time to get settled and to have supper before dark.

Across the street from the campground, there was a fresh foods market. Fresh fruits and vegetables were displayed in small wooden boxes on wooden tables. Double-decker buses stopped at the intersection there, transporting people to and from central London. The area was engulfed by old buildings. The campground was not large but was well established with an office and showers with concrete floors. Our site was in the middle of the camp.

That evening Sue Ellen's parents let us walk to a cinema several blocks from the campground. We didn't know what we were going to see, but we couldn't resist the opportunity to partake of local culture. We stood in line to buy our tickets with jeans-clad young people who smoked. When we walked into the theater, thick smoke was hanging from the ceiling. Our eyes burned, and for a moment, it was hard to breathe. It appeared that the entire theater was simmering in smoke, and when we sat down we noticed ashtrays on the back of each seat. As we looked around, we saw that almost everyone was smoking.

After the movie, we returned to the campsite to find her parents waiting at the entrance, looking for us. We unpacked our nightclothes and stood in line to use the shower. We met interesting people from all over Europe and heard many different languages. The shower was our local information exchange. We met the same people at the same time daily and exchanged tidbits of daily London adventures: where to go, what to see, who had the best food, and when to get the best prices. Not everyone we met spoke English. We took the tube into London daily to see the sights: Buckingham Palace and the changing of the guard; the Victoria and Albert Museum; Madam Tussaud's Wax Museum; Harrods, where I bought my father a red silk tie and my mother a box of sweet-smelling soap; and a riverboat tour of the Thames to Greenwich. I was especially glad that we walked through Trafalger Square several times. My father spoke about being in Trafalger Square and listening to people talk there during the war. He always had a smile on his face when he did, and he encouraged me to go there and see it, too. Sue Ellen and I only saw people passing quietly through the square, and a few old men sitting on the fountain edge feeding the pigeons. I wondered what there was about Trafalger Square that made my father smile so much, but when I reported that we had walked through the square several times, he was so pleased. After the morning tours, Sue Ellen's parents let us go our own way before noon while they went to a museum or back to the campsite.

We stopped in the makeup department at Harrods every day to speak with the glamorous, blonde-headed, blue-eyed saleslady who advised us about becoming glamorous without charging us. On our last day she gave us each a sample of the beautiful blue eye shadow she wore. Delighted and certain that with our free advice and free sample we would be among the most beautiful at Munich American High, we floated out of the heavy glass revolving doors onto the street to another adventure. We usually ate fish and chips at the same lunch counter, observing closely the young women who came in from work to eat and socialize. Would we become attractive working women with money to spend freely, or would we get married, have lots of children, and always need money? We discussed the pros and cons of both lifestyles over lunches. Sometimes we tried hamburgers on baps (white buns) like the young women who sat near us. After lunch we rode a double-decker bus around London and talked about all the people on the bus before getting back to the campsite in time for supper.

We loved being in London, hearing English wherever we were; driving in the country and through neighborhoods where the houses and yards were much like those in the States made us feel a little homesick. Most of all, we loved the British people. Sue Ellen and her parents were fun to be with and made me feel that I was a member of their family. On the way home to

Munich, we slept in the back of the Carmen Ghia, exhausted from our London adventures. It was my first camping trip and a wonderful experience. Sue Ellen and I remained the best of friends until my father was transferred back to the States in December of 1959.

1. My father, Frank, and I in the camel market in Tripoli, Lymbia. I am sixteen and Frank is twelve.
2. My father and I at the Acropolis in Athens.

The Mediterranean Cruise

Verona, Rome, Pompeii, Naples, Tripoli, Libya, Pireaus and Athens, Greece, Istanbul and Izmir, Turkey—these were our destinations in the handful of rolled papers my father brought home in late September 1959. We were going on a Mediterranean cruise. My mother complained about having to take a long trip before our return to the States in December, but my father was adamant that Frank and I should see this part of the world.

We drove to Verona, Italy, in one day and spent the night with our friends in their second-floor apartment. Natural light flooded every room through floor-to-ceiling windows; marble floors, counter tops, and a balcony for every window made it a wonderful place to live. Barbara and Bill, who was also a career army man, were my parents' best friends.

In December 1948, I'd stayed with them in Cheyenne, Wyoming, when Frank was born. In August, only a month before this trip, my parents let me spend two weeks with Barbara and Bill. I rode the bus to Lake Garda every day, where I learned to water ski. The beach was not crowded, and the few people I met were interested in speaking English. The sounds of *Folare*, a popular song, were playing everywhere I went. On the weekend, Barbara Ann, our friends' young daughter, and I walked to Juliet Capulet's tiny balcony. We stood with a small group of tourists, mostly English speaking, and listened to a docent talk about young Juliet.

Sometimes American tourists approached us to talk briefly. They were astonished to learn that Barbara Ann lived in

Verona with her parents, and I lived in Munich with mine. Most American tourists saved all their lives to travel to Verona for two weeks. I rode the train back to Munich by myself—from Verona through Austria, Switzerland, and finally, into Munich. The charming porter asked for tickets and made announcements in three languages. It was fun to speak with him in German and use what little Italian I had picked up. I knew just enough French to respond to a ticket agent. It was fun, and I wished I could live like this forever.

My father was waiting for me at the HauptBahnhof, the train station in downtown Munich. On the way home, he was very interested in the details of my trip. This was a rare opportunity to be with my father when he was relaxed, and I enjoyed being with him so much. I appreciated my parents letting me spend two weeks in Verona with Barbara and Bill.

During our September trip, we left Verona for Naples and the cruise. We stopped in Rome, and toured the Coliseum, built between AD 75 and 80. The maze of ruins on the ground confronted us with the reality of lions tearing humans apart for pleasure-watching Romans in concrete bleachers that seated 87,000 people. In Pompeii, we saw small houses with slits near the roof to let heat escape. We walked in the ruts left in narrow stone streets by old wagon wheels. Only men were allowed to tour one large house and came out blushing, rattling the change in their pockets while women and children stood in the heat, wondering what was so interesting inside. We saw the petrified remains of food in dishes still on the table. The writhing forms of a young girl and a dog, both encased in volcanic ash, showed that the people of Pompeii had suffered tragic deaths.

In the lingering heat we boarded the MSTS ship in Naples and pulled away from the harbor, heading across the Mediterranean to Tripoli, Libya. Sometimes my parents stood on deck, searching the horizon for land or studying the beautiful blue Mediterranean Sea, while Frank and I stood close by. When we disembarked at Tripoli and walked down the gangplank, the heat nearly knocked us out. The odor from the camel market and camel urine in the gutters was overwhelming. As we rode into the city, we saw incredible wealth and incredible poverty, but no evidence of a middle class. Some people were dressed in long robes with their heads covered to protect them from the sun. We saw beggars in the gutters covered head to toe in white robes. Each one had evidence of a missing body part—toes, fingers, a hand—a disfigured face, or no teeth. I was astonished to see groups of white-robed men—human beings—sitting in the gutters running yellow and green with camel urine and other refuse, where the odors were especially strong.

Our first stop was at the camel market, where nearly a hundred thin and scruffy looking Arabian camels that appeared to be losing their coats lounged in a large empty lot. These camels were not related to the pampered animals we saw in the zoo. Prospective buyers walked around the roped off area, showing interest in a specific camel. The owner stepped into the herd and pulled out the designated animal for the prospective buyer to inspect. Camels screeched to each other, to their owners, and to prospective buyers. Like a cattleman, the interested buyer stroked the animal, feeling its girth, and inspecting its legs, hooves, eyes, and teeth before it was returned to the herd. Buyers were not in a hurry that day and could not be persuaded by the owner to buy.

Poverty greeted us as we drove toward the city. Barefooted children, ragged and dirty, lived in the squalor of crumbling apartments surrounded by rubble and refuse. In the oppressive heat, people were pressed into the smallest spaces without overhead covering to escape a blistering sun. There were also large, white, dome-shaped buildings with beautiful arches, fronted by palm trees, fountains, and ponds. Observing overwhelming poverty and overwhelming wealth in the same glance was startling, unsettling, and unbelievable. As we continued into the city, someone on the bus said loudly, "That's where the Italians lived in WWII."

"Looks like they're still there."

"Hey, Mussolini was here during the war."

"Two times," somebody else shouted.

Finally, we arrived in the Madinah, the old city, near the harbor. There were colorful shops there, layered, one on top of the other. Many of the shopkeepers lived above their shops. Before we left the bus, the American military guide warned us to stay together in groups and not to wander away from the main streets. Prior to our visit, several GIs had been knifed and murdered in broad daylight. Beautiful tile work covering the floor and the walls inside the shops drew us in, regardless of the warnings we'd just been given. We wandered the narrow, winding streets into an open door. Silver jewelry and Libyan *objets d'art* were artfully displayed. A few local residents were browsing inside the shop.

The middle-aged woman behind the counter had thick, black, tousled curls and wore a Western-style print dress. When she looked up suddenly and noticed us, she screamed, "What do you want!" Glaring at us she screamed again, "What do you want!" Everyone in the shop turned to stare, and no one was smiling. The woman's black eyes threw daggers at us. Stunned at this unexpected address, my father looked directly at her with his most charming smile. We walked toward the open door, smiling as we left, while the Libyan shoppers continued to glare at us. We wandered silently for a while, heading in a different direction, and then we came to a shop filled with maroon fezzes. Frank wanted to try one on. He kept tossing his head left and right, making the white tassel swing around and around. My father helped him find one that fit his head and bought it. Frank was delighted. The shopkeeper was pleased with the sale, but he never smiled. We were satisfied to leave and be on the street again.

It was getting hotter. I was thirsty and feeling hungry. I walked behind Frank and my parents, watching everyone and everything to make sure we were not being followed while taking in as much of the Madinah as my eyes could hold. We were only a short distance from the bus and soon fell in with other passengers.

I walked ahead now to make sure the bus was still in the same place. A line was forming at the door, and each person in line had at least one shopping bag. I looked back where my parents and Frank had been walking, but I couldn't see them. Passengers were still boarding the bus. Remembering the story of the GIs who had been knifed and murdered a few days prior to our visit, I began to worry. When we left the dock, every seat had been filled. My parents and Frank were nowhere to be seen. I panicked and started to run back to the silver shop where we were so rudely addressed, but people on the bus yelled at me through the windows.

"Hey, we're leaving now. You better get on the bus! The shopping's over!" The noonday heat was bearing down, and the bus riders were anxious to get away, to feel the wind blowing through the windows while the bus was moving. The driver revved the engine loudly.

"My parents aren't here! I have to find my parents!" I yelled. I had to find my parents and my brother, but they were looking for me too.

"Mary Lou! Mary Lou! Where are you going?" my father shouted through one of the windows. "Mary Lou!" my mother shouted.

Tears welled in my eyes. I headed for the open door of the bus. The driver looked indignant as I climbed up the stairs. Applause sprinkled throughout the bus as I looked for the empty seat Frank was saving for me.

"At last," somebody said loudly. "It's about time," someone else mumbled as I passed by. I was so humiliated. Why did my parents board the bus without me?

After we started moving, my father turned to me and said sharply, "Mary Lou, why don't you pay attention from now on. Huh?"

"Why didn't you get on the bus?" my mother asked, curious.

"I thought you were lost. I couldn't find you any place. I was going to find you," I said softly. "I thought you would wait for me at the bus; when I didn't see you, I went to find you." Some people sitting near us thought the whole scene was very funny and laughed. My parents turned around silently.

The bus headed for the base, the largest one we had ever seen. For security reasons, there were two checkpoints to pass through instead of the usual one. Due to the extreme heat every building was air-conditioned. In the delicatessen we ate hamburgers and french fries. We ordered Cokes with ice, but there wasn't any ice, so we drank hot Coke and lukewarm water. Afterward, we went into the large PX, where I bought a silver camel charm for my charm bracelet like many of the other women in our group. Soon we were boarding the bus again and were on our way back to the dock. That night we were on our way to Piraeus and Athens, Greece. So far I had not been seasick. I hoped to avoid it for the rest of the trip.

The intense blue of the Mediterranean was still fascinating to me because the water was so clear and I could see white rocks on the bottom. We passed small islands scattered off the coast of Greece as we headed for Piraeus and Athens. As we docked, merchants were unpacking their wares to sell to the Americans. When we disembarked, passengers wandered over to see the colorful amphorae, pots, urns, dishes, jewelry, and clothing displayed by friendly English-speaking merchants.

We boarded a bus and headed into Athens. Along the way, I was again shocked to see incredible poverty. Heaps of rubble from WWII lined the roadside. Small shacks had been created from the rubble and large cardboard boxes, which served as the roofs, windows, and doors. Some hovels were made entirely of cardboard.

We could see the Acropolis above the city as we approached Athens. The bus stopped first in Athens, where people greeted us warmly everywhere we went. Merchants and clerks in the stores were very friendly. We went into a café for something to drink and the smiling proprietor came over to speak to us. After some coffee for my parents and Coke with ice for Frank and me, we boarded the bus once again and headed up to the Temple of Athena and the Parthenon.

Our guide spoke in such detail about Greek history that I couldn't listen to her after a while. I stepped back on the uneven sun-bleached stones absorbing the remains of great society. No one spoke of the human toll spent to achieve the beauty surrounding us. Now I understood what Frau Hellerer was talking about. Take in the culture where you are; then you will have something to talk about. It didn't matter that I didn't have a boyfriend and wasn't dating anyone. I didn't care whether my clothes were stylish or not. It didn't matter if I were not a popular high-school student. I had something greater that wouldn't fade. Something that would endure, but I couldn't put it in words. Extraordinary remains of antiquity surrounded me. I had walked in the footsteps of remarkable thinkers like Aristotle and Sophocles and seen structures designed by some of the earliest architects. My need to be accepted as a popular student faded in the shadows of the Parthenon.

At the conclusion of our tour on the Acropolis, we walked through aisles of uneven concrete benches in the open-air amphitheater carved into the side of the mountain. The midday sun bore down as a guide proved the acoustics in the amphitheater were perfect. Standing on the stage while our group stood or sat on the benches, he spoke quietly, but his voice sounded as if he were standing directly in front of us. We could clearly hear and understand everything he said. Quietly the group returned to the bus. As we descended the Acropolis and studied the tiled rooftops of Athens, I wondered what it must have been like when Aristotle walked these streets. When we reached Pireaus, passengers flocked to the merchants who had set up their wares early in the morning, each one hoping to find a perfect copy of the ancient society where democracy was born, a souvenir that would prompt a memory of a day spent in the shadows of the Acropolis.

On our way to Istanbul, Turkey, the next stop, I looked down at the clear blue water of the Mediterranean Sea from the ship's deck, studied the loose rocks on the sea floor, and wondered about Socrates and Aristotle.

My father bought this ring for my mother in the Grand Bazaar, Istanbul, Turkey.

The Amethyst Ring

Open coffee shops, men wearing vests, and smoking narghile (a Turkish water pipe) greeted us as we disembarked in Istanbul. Next to each group of men was a large glass container. The bottom was filled with water, and the top was an assortment of snaking fabric tubes leading from the glass container to a pipe the men inhaled.

We drove over the Golden Horn to the Blue Mosque and Topkapi Palace. Along the way, the driver stopped and pointed out the Bosphorus Strait and, beyond that, Asia. At Topkapi Palace, we found the harem especially interesting. The guide informed us that the queen mother chose young women for the king. The living quarters were beautiful, filled with light, and appeared to be very comfortable. We saw sacred relics belonging to Mohammed and his followers as well as historic remnants of the Ottoman Empire.

We removed our shoes and left them at the door with everyone else's before entering the Blue Mosque, hoping they would be there when we returned. As I recall, the stunning interior walls were covered with small pieces of blue tiles. Rays of light poured through large, arched windows onto blue-velvet kneeling pillows that covered the floor. A tall, white-domed ceiling added to the simple beauty. I stood by myself and studied the architecture, the walls, the windows, and the ceiling while offering some silent prayers.

We had about two hours to spend in the Grand Bazaar. Although electric light bulbs hung from simple cords over some of the stalls, it was still very dark inside. The bazaar was crowded with people who were intent on finding the best price, the best deal, or a certain spice. We wandered in, afraid of getting lost and never coming out. We had the day to explore Istanbul and had to return to the ship by six o'clock that evening. There would be no time or excuse for getting lost. My father sternly warned us to stay together.

It was incredibly hot outside, but inside the bazaar, it was even hotter because it was packed with people, all moving, buying, eating, and searching for the best bargain. Humidity clung to us like glue. None of this seemed to affect the native shoppers. My parents were not avid shoppers, but we wandered the narrow, irregular aisles in search of some special souvenir from Istanbul. We passed the leather stalls with everything imaginable made of leather, clothing stalls with beautiful fabrics, scarves, and embroidered silks. My mother noticed a booth with all kinds of pipes and bought a meerschaum pipe for Uncle Edward. I found some Turkish slippers with turned-up toes and embroidered decoration on top. "What are you going to do with those?" my father asked me. "I can wear them in the house," I replied. He rolled his eyes but didn't say anything else.

Then we turned a dark corner, and there was more gold jewelry than the eye could behold, even in the darkness of the bazaar. My mother had a good eye for quality. She dressed well even when she went to the grocery store. To my father, she was like an orchid in the desert. He was a man of good taste and was anxious to find something special for her. She had good hands with long, narrow fingers. Her fingernails were always polished, and she wore rings every day. So they looked through displays of gold rings after the smiling English-speaking merchant convinced my parents that he had the best bargains. My mother tried on several rings, but the one-inch-square amethyst in a simple gold setting looked so beautiful on her ring finger that it was a done deal before she could even take it off. In fact, she wore it out of the bazaar after some bargaining between my father and the merchant. He was so pleased to buy this ring for her, and she was delighted to be wearing it.

Although our family was from the South, the oppressive heat and humidity took a toll on us, and we headed for the bus, hoping that everyone else from the ship would do the same. Instead, we sat and sat and sat. Sweat beaded, dripped, and then ran down our skin until our clothes were sticking to us. Eventually a few other travelers climbed silently on board. There must have been nearly ten people on board when I looked at the door, hoping that others would be coming from the bazaar so we could leave. The moving bus would generate enough humid air to bring some relief from the clinging heat and our sticky clothes.

Instead of passengers, there was a dark-skinned young man standing on the stump of his knees, timidly holding out his left hand. There were no legs or feet below his knees. His right hand held on to the chrome door frame of the bus. He wore a dark-red, short-sleeved shirt with an open collar, with no signs of perspiration or wrinkles, and clean gray pants folded at the knees. He held himself up on the stumps of his legs like a rod and said nothing, but his piercing black eyes begged for help, for money, for food. Everyone on the bus looked away, avoiding his presence. There was competition between the passengers on the bus to see who could outlast the other in avoiding the beggar. Sweat beads rolled down our foreheads. My heart ached for the young man. I tried not to look at him, but he was so pitiful, so helpless, his eyes so intense, that his calm, quiet energy drew me into his beautiful black eyes.

My father told us that Americans were often tested this way to guarantee that money was not given to the black market or that we were not harmed by an underground person who hated Americans. I rationalized that must be the reason no one moved forward to help this young man. I dared not move in his direction because my parents would openly disapprove, which would be even more humiliating for the young man. My heart ached for him, and I couldn't stop staring at him. My father took notice of this and coughed slightly to get my attention. He frowned briefly at me while nodding his head in the direction of the young man. I looked away and out of the window at shoppers moving in and out of the bazaar. After sometime, he slowly, but deliberately removed himself from the bus with difficulty, but without any alms from the Americans.

The last of the passenger ambled from the Grand Bazaar, packages in hand, and boarded the bus. The driver closed the door and started the engine. We pulled away from the fascinating shopping mecca teeming with people and goods and headed for the ship and the next port of call.

After returning to the staterooms and storing purchases, passengers returned to the deck to watch the departure. We picked up some extra passengers from the American community in Istanbul. I noticed a young woman and her husband standing close together on deck, waving to her parents on shore. As the ship pulled away from shore, tears ran down her cheeks while she stared at her parents. Rumor on board was that they were newlyweds.

As we headed out to sea, the American flag on shore waved in the late-afternoon breeze. The sun began to set, throwing a beautiful array of colors on this ancient land. As we passed in front of the Stars and Stripes, every passenger stood with the right hand over the heart and watched in silence while the flag grew smaller and smaller. The sun sank lower into the horizon as the ship moved slowly toward the Aegean Sea and Izmir.

I remember few details about being in Izmir, other than it was much smaller than Istanbul, and the pace of life seemed to be more relaxed and slower. We did tour a market, but there was no comparison to the Grand Bazaar. After we left Izmir, our final stop, we returned to Naples.

My parents located our car and packed it with goods from the trip. It was a good trip even though my mother hadn't wanted to go. As we left Naples, we stopped at a nearby marble quarry. My parents were as fascinated with the marble as they were with the extraction process. A large square of black marble with dark green running diagonally across it captured their eyes. It took two men to lift it into the trunk of our light blue '56 ford. Frank and I wondered how they would get it out of the trunk and up the stairs to our second-floor apartment when we returned to Munich. My father had a sturdy wooden frame made, and the marble became our coffee table.

On our way back to Munich, we made one last stop, in Pisa to see the Leaning Tower. In the heat of a late September afternoon, we stood and stared at the famous tower. It certainly did lean. It was leaning from every direction one might look. The tower itself was beautiful, and so was the marble courtyard surrounding it. I wondered what it might have been like to climb the stairs all the way to the top. I didn't have much time to wonder, however, because my father was anxious to get to Verona. We walked to the car and climbed in with memories of a wonderful trip that had exposed us to historical times and places, fascinating cultures, great successes of ancient leaders, the tragic remains of horrible wars, and the enduring qualities of humankind.

This picture was taken in front of our apartment building in Perlacher Forst, Munich. I'm wearing the dress my mother made for my initiation into the Rainbow Girls. I wore this dress when my father danced with me on the SS America, in December 1959. I was sixteen.

SS America

In the late 1950s, President Eisenhower declared the "human war machine" was no longer necessary and ordered a reduction of manpower in the armed forces. My father was one of those numbers, and in December 1959, we were on our way to the States for the last time. The prospect of not moving again was unsettling. It was the only life Frank and I knew. What would it be like living in the States again? What would it be like living with people who had always lived in the same place and knew nothing about life and culture overseas? My father didn't know what he would do after he retired, which was very unsettling for both of my parents, although they didn't talk about it with us.

In early December we arrived in Bremerhaven by train. Under our winter coats we were dressed in layers of wool sweaters, skirts, and pants, we were not prepared for the bitterly cold wind blowing off the North Sea and the chill from snow-packed streets and sidewalks. At the time, women did not wear pants, but we saw beautiful women, dressed in layers and knee-high boots, moving about on the streets of Bremerhaven with bright red knees due to the cold, sharp wind. None of us could ever remember such bone-chilling cold. It took us three days to warm up after we boarded the ship.

We boarded the SS *America* and headed across the English Channel to Southampton, England, where we disembarked for a few hours. Near the ship my father found a cabbie who had lived through the last war. He was more than willing to give us a tour of the area. My father and the cabbie sat in the front seat and had great conversations about the war years, while the cabbie drove us to the shipyard where the English battleship *George V* was moored, and the marked spot where the Pilgrims left for America. When we returned to the dock after a couple of hours, my father gave him a generous tip. They shook hands warmly and seemed reluctant to part company. At the time, I did not know my father had been to Southampton many times during the war.

The enormous SS *America* was beautiful and luxurious throughout. This was the only time we did not travel by sea on a military ship. My parents and Frank were assigned a cabin of their own. I found my name on the cabin next door. At sixteen, I was old enough to share a room with an adult. The middle-aged woman who shared the cabin with me was head librarian for American schools in Germany. Miss Sharon George was single and befriended me in the warmest of ways. We shared a love of books, and I spent hours reading in my top bunk bed while she never moved from her place or said a word. In particular, I read *Les Miserables* while on board. One evening, she invited me to join her for dinner at the captain's table, her regular table assignment. Our French waiter spoke with such a heavy accent, I could hardly understand him, but he was a superb waiter, anticipating one's every need. The conversation of professional people around the table fascinated me.

Outside a hard, cold wind scattered salt spray up on the deck. Huge waves crashed against the side of the ship. Staying outside on the main deck for more than a few minutes was risky. I pushed hard on the steel door and entered the lobby. My shoes sank into the plush carpet. Sipping hot drinks and smoking, a few well-dressed passengers lounged comfortably in velvet club chairs, watching salt spray spatter against the windows. In the center of the room, chairs and tables set with china and silverware glowed in the dimmed overhead light of large crystal chandeliers. I passed unnoticed through the salon and exited into a passageway leading to my stateroom. Holding the handrail, I steadied myself against the roll of the ship as I made my way down the long hallway. I pushed on the steel door and entered the stateroom.

Dressed only in a slip, Miss Sharon sat at the dressing table, brushing her hair. "You look cold, Mary Lou," she said. "You didn't stay out long. Are you going to dinner?"

I sank into the lower bunk and removed my heavy coat, gloves, and scarf. "Yes," I said. "It is cold, but I'm going to have dinner. I'm starved. I think I'll wear my wool dress tonight because it has long sleeves, and I'm freezing. I hope the dinner is something I like."

Miss Sharon smiled as she applied rouge to her cheeks. "Are you going to shower before you get dressed?" she asked.

"No, I don't think so," I said. "I was only outside for a few minutes, but I'm chilled from standing in the wind."

We dressed for dinner, exited the stateroom, holding on to the handrail in the wide hallway, and headed for the elegant dining salon. As we entered and moved unnoticed to a long table near the middle of the room, the orchestra was playing a Strauss waltz. Large crystal chandeliers dazzled in the soft glow of evening light. At the head of the table, an elegant-looking man with silver hair, dressed in a tuxedo, spoke animatedly to diners seated left and right of him. Miss Sharon informed me that he was the ship's captain. Our French-speaking waiter seated us, greeted other guests seated near us, and took our drink orders—a glass of red wine for Miss Sharon and hot tea for me. We read the beautifully decorated menu while waiting for our attentive waiter to take orders.

I looked across the room and noticed my parents and Frank smiling at me. I smiled and nodded in return. My father was wearing his dark-blue dress uniform with gold trim and gold buttons. My mother was wearing a black taffeta dress with a large green plaid on it. She bought the fabric in Japan and had the dress made. Frank was dressed in his Sunday clothes with a white shirt, a bow tie, a sport coat, and dress pants. I wore the ice-blue taffeta dress with a pumpkin skirt my mother made for my initiation into the Rainbow Girls.

After dinner I thanked Miss Sharon for inviting me to dine with her at the captain's table and excused myself to join my parents in another salon where a band was playing. Miss Sharon left with others at the table for more conversation and coffee in the bar. My parents and Frank were sitting at a small table for four people, not far from the stage. Since I was staying in a room with another adult, I had been feeling older than sixteen and chose to sit with a friend not far from my parents and Frank. Easy dancing music by Benny Goodman, Glenn Miller, and Frank Sinatra kept the dance floor crowded. My parents moved easily to Glenn Miller's "String of Pearls." They looked so happy and elegant; Frank and I watched proudly. They returned to the table and sat for a moment longer, sipping their drinks, rum and Coke. I noticed my father looking at me and smiling.

The little girl he once knew had grown into a young woman of sixteen. He didn't seem to know me, sitting there wearing a semiformal dress and white sandal-style heels that I bought in Italy. I was surprised when he came over to my table and asked me to dance. We danced slowly and not very well, but we danced. I saw my mother smiling at us out of the corner of my eye. Frank sat close to her, watching us dance. My father stared at me silently while we danced. His face had such a warm glow. He was proud of me, and it showed. He wasn't "war ready," he wasn't fighting a war, and he wasn't ordering his troops around. He just held me and danced slowly until the music ended. Then he walked me back to the table and pulled out a chair for me.

After my father sat down, he looked at me for a long time, and then he took a sip of his drink. My mother sat quietly and smiled at him. *Where had all those years gone when I was growing up and he was away?* I was a young lady now. Maybe my father was wondering the same thing. He looked at me through a smile, but his eyes had a sad, faraway look. We never shared another moment like that, and when I go to heaven, it will still be in my heart. I wondered why there couldn't have been more times like this, just the two of us, my father and me. I wish I could have known him when he wasn't as angry as a caged lion. I wish I could have known better the man who just danced with me. Sitting at separate tables, Frank and I listened to the band play and watched the dancing. In a moment, my father came over with Frank and told me we needed to return to our stateroom. My parents stayed in the salon, listening to the music, reflecting on our life in Munich, and wondering what our future in the States might be like. Later they joined a small group at a larger table.

The next morning, I sat at a small desk in an alcove off the salon of the ship. A few other passengers sat here and there at desks, absorbed in thought or in writing. On top of each writing table there was a small wooden box holding stationery with "SS *America*" printed at the top. My mother approached as I was writing. Bending down, she whispered to me, "The man sitting across from you is Salvador Dalí."

I looked up and saw an older man with slick black hair combed straight back and lightly tanned skin. He was wearing a white shirt, a light-gray vest, and suit jacket. A pencil mustache, waxed so heavily it appeared to be glued onto his upper lip, was an outstanding characteristic of the man's physical makeup. He was looking directly me. I was embarrassed and turned my head. After a moment, I asked my mother, "Who is Salvador Dalí?"

"A famous artist," she whispered. I took another glance over the top of the writing desk. Salvador Dalí was still looking at me intently. I looked down at my letters and showed my mother what I had written to my friends in Munich.

"That's very nice," she replied in a low voice. "I'll be in the salon when you finish." I continued to write but noticed that Salvador Dalí and his pencil mustache were still staring at me. His intense attention made me nervous, so I turned to my letters again. I thought about the Christmas Eve we spent with the Gruckenberg family only a week earlier. I remembered Jon Madsen fondly and how he used to help me with my German homework. There was the trip to Berchtesgaden for the Red Cross Leadership Camp and the camping trip to London with Sue Ellen and her family. *Will I ever return to Germany? What will my life in the States be like?* Sadness washed over me. I felt pulled between two places at the same time. In three days we would dock in New York. If only I could have stayed in Munich, but who could I have lived with? I didn't want to leave Germany, but I could hardly wait to see my grandparents in Houston. *Who am I now? Where do I belong?* I finished my letters to friends in Munich and one to my grandparents. I returned to the main deck, looking for seagulls and signs of land. The cold wind whipped salt spray hard against the side of the ship. It was impossible to stay outside on the main deck for more than a few minutes at a time.

Our arrival in New York marked the end of our military life. When we docked and walked down the gangplank, we stepped onto the same land my great-grandparents and great-great-grandparents came to, hoping to find a better life for themselves. My paternal relatives came from Wales and Holland. My maternal great-grandparents came from London and Darmstadt. My German relatives entered the United States through Ellis Island, and now we were docking in New York Harbor. I wondered how they felt when they disembarked and stepped on this new land. *What hopes and dreams did they all bring with them? Did they ever regret coming here?* It hardly seemed possible that we were in the States again. Ten day earlier we left Bremerhaven and made a day stop in Southampton. Collecting our luggage, getting our car, finding our way out of the harbor area, we felt like strangers in our own country. As we drove through New York City, we stared silently, taking in the strange sights, sounds, and smells of a large American city. I wondered ... *what will it be like to be an American living in America again?*

Frank with my parents in the living room of our house in Bellaire before he left for Fort Polk, Louisana, and later Chu Lai, Vietnam.

Epilogue

We lived an extraordinary life, experiencing cultures on both sides of the world in ways that many people will never know. In Alaska, we experienced two earthquakes and saw the northern lights. Living in the old house in downtown Nara was an unforgettable time. Our lives were greatly enriched by Mama-san, Mr. and Mrs. Kimoto, and our beloved Hatsie. My life was especially enlarged by the kindness of the Japanese students in Nara, who extended themselves in such a caring way to a lost and very lonely American child. Mr. and Mrs. Gruckenberg, Helga, and Gerhard were like family to us. Without them we would never have really known Munich or the radiant warmth of the German people. Jon Madsen, my father's good friend, shared his family in Copenhagen with us and later came to see us in the States. Living in Nara and traveling throughout Europe and the Mediterranean helped us to understand the historical advancement of humankind, while at the same time, witnessing powerful forces of human destruction. Our values and our horizons were broadened considerably by these experiences, but the long, gripping tentacles of war reached far and deep into our family life.

Being a military dependent left me with a strong need for order and the feeling that I do not belong in any one place. Change is the norm for me, but for people around me, stability is the norm. Repetitive behaviors remain the most challenging for me. I still struggle with issues of abandonment and rejection.

When my life as a military dependent ended, I had to assimilate into American life. I had to learn how to be a civilian, how to live in one place, how to make and keep friends, and how to work out difficulties. Prior to this, my life consisted of always starting over; there was never any ending.

After reading my father's WWII diary for this book, I was absolutely astonished to learn what he had experienced and endured during WWII as a young soldier. As an adult looking back over my childhood, I can see now that his war experiences as a young man affected him throughout his life. I am grateful for his strength and admire deeply the courage he demonstrated in life. He had a good heart and helped many people, civilians and military, throughout his life. From him I learned to withstand adversity, to be a strong person, and to not be afraid of life. My mother was very good with people and enabled us to communicate successfully with people who did not speak English. She helped us befriend wonderful people when we would otherwise have been very alone. As a military wife she created a warm and comfortable home wherever we lived from army-issue furniture. She entertained often and graciously.

After living in St. James, Missouri, for six months, where my father officially retired from the army at Fort Leonard Wood, we settled in Houston. My father started a landscaping business that later became a small construction company. My mother made a career at Trinity Universal Insurance Company. My brother and I both graduated from Bellaire High School. I went to Stephen F. Austin State University and he joined the Army. On April 6, 1978, my father died of lung cancer at fifty-eight. A twenty-year veteran and army engineer, he was honored for service to this country with a military salute at his funeral. Shortly after his death, my mother was diagnosed with Alzheimer's disease. Eight years later, on April 6, 1986, she passed away at sixty-two. Constantly relocating had robbed my parents of living a stable life while giving my brother and me the opportunity to travel and experience history and fascinating cultures throughout the world.

About the Author

Photo by Curtis Polk

Mary Lou Darst was born in Houston, Texas, and while growing up, traveled the world as a military dependent. She attended Stephen F. Austin State University, married, and moved to Galveston, Texas, where she learned to live in one place for the first time in her life. She returned to school twenty-eight years later and earned a bachelor of arts in literature, a master's of science in multicultural studies, and a bachelor of arts in visual and applied design. She taught English language arts and English as a second language in public schools and three community colleges.

She has a son, a daughter, two grandsons, a stepdaughter, and four grand-dogs. She lives in the Houston area with her partner, Peter, whose understanding, patience, and editorial support made this book a reality.

CPSIA information can be obtained
at www.ICGtesting.com
Printed in the USA
FSHW020235190719
60139FS